Just tell me when you're gonna stick me!

An Ordinary Man

An Extraordinary Life

A Fighting Chance

Anthony D. Rabak

Anastasia —

Thank you for taking
good care of me during
my time at RSI —
You are a gifted and
caring nurse.
You make a difference.
    Best Wishes
    — Anthony

Jeremiah
29-11-13

TABLE OF CONTENTS

—☙☙☙—

Introduction

What you are about to read is a product of much encouragement, first from my lovely wife and then from many people who have allowed me the privilege of sharing my life experiences with them. This is not fiction — it is true.

When my wife first presented the idea of writing a book about my life, my initial reaction was "NO, why would anyone want to read about me?" Yet, despite my hesitancy she kept encouraging me. At some point someone else also said to me, "You should write a book about your life", and my response was an appreciative yet dismissive, "Yeah, that's what my wife says." Soon after that someone else expressed the same thing, and then came another encouragement, and another, then another, and so on.

Since several people were telling me the same thing, I finally mentioned to God in a mental prayer my hesitancy and asked, "Why would anyone want to read a book about me and my life?" The response to my inquiry was an eye-opener. "This will not be a book about YOU; it will be about ME and what I've done in your life!"

I humbly yielded and you now hold the result in your hands. As I began to see the story of my life in ink, I could see clearly that this is not about me alone or any accomplishments I've attained. I truly have been just a passenger on a journey, and I have so enjoyed the ride so far. I look forward to whatever lies ahead.

Thank you for the opportunity to share with you what He has done for me. This is my testimony; the events of which I am a witness. People may say, "I don't know how to share a testimony!" Well, if you are called into court and asked to testify, you are merely being asked to share that which you have seen or to share something about which you have expertise, experience, or first hand knowledge of. That is a testimony, and here is mine...

Prologue

A mental image repeated showing a perfectly clear picture window which framed a view of my life. Recent circumstances acted as a large brick that had been thrown, causing thousands of shards of glass to come crashing to the ground. This brick, sadly, was tossed by *my own* hands.

Previously, at times when my life was pelted by minor pebbles and stones, I always managed to find a way to repair, or at least conceal, the minor chips and cracks; but this...

I saw no way I could handle this. I felt nothing but despair and hopelessness. I had always managed to find a way out of problems before but faced with all these little pieces of glass, I couldn't even begin to see where to start. A condemning soundtrack kept repeating as to how I had really screwed things up this time and that there was no way I could fix this.

What was I going to do? A thought came to me. *Suicide?* Absolutely NOT! Sure, that would end my problems, but after 12 years of parochial school and an enjoyment of playing a popular board game — I had this to say, *"If you take your own life, you will not pass 'Go', you don't collect $200. You go straight to Jail!"*

My mind raced with utter confusion as this tormenting 'footage' of breaking glass kept replaying in my mind. Taking a step back from this, it suddenly dawned on me what I was doing. I was taking a drive to clear my head and analyze the situation, which was something I'd done countless times before. This revelation, though, was not in what I was physically doing at that moment in time but in where I was and *what* I was driving; my cherished 1968 Chevrolet Camaro with a newly transplanted high performance and hot-rodded engine that could go real fast. I could easily drive up from Davis where I was attending school to the Sierra Mountains where it was currently snowing. If it happened, I theorized, while taking a drive on a snowy mountain highway that I should happen to lose control of this powerful muscle car and career off the road, *that* wouldn't be suicide; it would be a tragic *accident,* and my problems would be over. I find it interesting how the devil will try new angles with us when attempting to throw us off the course that God has planned for us.

I determined that *my* plan was worth pursuing (or at least contemplating further while I drove), so I started for the freeway and the on-ramp towards the mountains; Interstate Highway 80 *East.* Then a phenomenon that most driving individuals have experienced at one time or another happened. I describe it as sort of a mental time warp; while caught up in a state of deep thought, you unknowingly lose sense of your immediate surroundings and time until a moment of clarity hits you and you realize that while on 'Auto-Pilot' you have no recollection of the last few miles of driving. Well, when my moment of lucidity hit me, I realized that I was, indeed, on Highway 80 but heading the wrong direction!

Chapter 1

The Beginning

——⟨ⱨⱨⱨ⟩——

My Dad is an awesome man! The oldest son in a family of eight, he was born in Istria, a small, fertile peninsula between Italy and the former Yugoslavia; now modern day Croatia. Having grown up very poor, he had adolescent dreams of escaping the bonds of communism and getting to the "land of milk and honey"; a far off place he'd heard of called the United States where some relatives lived and from where wonderful "care packages" would come. At the age of 17 he risked his life to escape over the border with another young man into neighboring Italy. It was while in a refugee camp that he heard of an opportunity to gain passage to Canada in exchange for one year of labor on a farm. Dad knew it wasn't the U.S. but at least it was the right continent. He came here not knowing the language and with only the clothes he was wearing and spare change in his pockets. After his service on the farm with minimal pay, he then worked several jobs while attending night school to learn English. At each job he used natural aptitude and learned new skills rapidly as he worked and got schooling where he could to advance from general labor to becoming a machine operator, then to a technician in both the electrical and electronics industries. It was while he was going to school that he attended a dance at an ethnic hall that my mother also happened to attend with one of her close friends (at her mother's urging). That night Angela met Dario, and they were married 18 months later.

Their family started in Canada where my older sister Marie and my brother Frank were born. Mom knew Dad's dream was to go to America but Dad knew that as the only daughter in a strict Italian family, Mom was very close to her parents and was resolved to always living near them. He didn't push the issue. After 12 years of marriage, an opportunity was then presented to start a life in California, and my mom was surprisingly okay with it. A relative of my father who was living in California offered to sell him a business there, a liquor store. My folks had previously bought and operated Ted's Washing Machines in Ontario, Canada, so running a business was not new to them. Although it was not something in my dad's previous line of work, this was an opportunity to see his dreams fulfilled, so they both agreed to give it a try. My parents sold everything, packed up their young family and set out on their bold new future. Once in California, the relative changed their mind and decided not to sell them the business after all. Talk about pulling the rug out from under your feet! This became the incentive that led to my folks taking their capital and starting Dario's Appliance, selling and servicing major home appliances. This was something they were more familiar with and their endeavor became a very successful fixture in their new community. Ironically, the liquor store that led them to California subsequently became victim to looting and vandalism during a city riot that had broken out.

Things were going well in the life of my parents but one day Mom felt a little under the weather and thought she might be coming down with the flu. A trip to the doctor clarified it; she wasn't sick. At the age of 39 she learned she was pregnant! Turned out she had the nine month flu. Dad was elated! Another dream of his was to have a child born in America. It seemed the future was looking bright for my family. For my father, it was his California dream coming true.

Shortly thereafter, my mom got the news that her mother was sick with cancer. During her pregnancy she made several trips back to Canada to be with her mom.

In between she was trying to be a "good Catholic", attending Mass, lighting candles, and saying prayers for her mom. Still, her mother got worse and died before I was born. This caused Mom to get mad at God because she felt that He had ignored her prayers.

My parents focused on their new life in California. Dad became consumed with work and desired to become a successful businessman motivated by the desire to provide a better life for his children than he had growing up. Mom devoted herself to being Dad's business partner, a hard worker, faithful wife and a loving mother.

Chapter 2

Why Him?

———

When I was little, my parents' neighbor would watch me while my folks were working. She was like an "aunt" to me; actually, she became like a second mom. She began to be concerned for me because I was loosing my appetite and seemed very pale. Mom took me to our family doctor. His conclusion was that I seemed anemic, which was treatable. He instructed my mother to give me iron supplements for three months and then bring me back for a follow-up visit at that time. My folks were advised that that they could go ahead and take a planned trip to Europe; that I would be fine left in my older sister's care until they returned.

Many people have heroes: Batman, Superman, Wonder-Woman, etc. I'm no exception I guess, but mine is not a fictional character. My hero was and is my father. An early childhood remembrance I have is in 1974 at the age of five. I often was found by my dad's side in some sort of mirroring of his actions. This particular day he was engaged in what most would consider an un-heroic task of building a backyard chicken coop (a 'hen-house')! Nonetheless, there I was with toy hammer in hand, pounding at imaginary nails in an attempt to try and keep up with every swing of my dad's. Suddenly, I became very tired and in frustration threw down my 'tool' and headed back to the house. With my dad at my side, he questioned Mom as to what exactly the doctor had said. My father decided that they both needed to go and speak with this doctor. He was not going to go on their trip until they were sure I was ok. Fortunately, the doctor referred me to the hospital for blood tests.

On April 24, 1974 my parents were immediately told to go to Children's Hospital in Oakland. After another quick set of tests, my parents were given the preliminary diagnosis. All indications seemed to point to leukemia, which is a blood cancer. They immediately checked me into the hospital and were told they'd have a more definite diagnosis once a bone marrow test was performed. My folk's trip was postponed.

Mom was further pushed into her distance from God, still raw and bitter dealing with the death of her mom from cancer when she was seven months pregnant with me. My parents were expectedly stunned by this trau-matic revelation. My father said every time he closed his eyes he was haunted by an image of a small white casket being lowered into the ground. My mom's only thoughts were, "Why him? Why him? He's so young, so innocent!" Mom had since given up on praying when she felt her prayers went unanswered for her mom.

The next day came the finding that I had a blood hemoglobin reading of 7 (a normal childhood level being 12-14). The official diagnosis now was acute lymphoblastic leukemia. My condition was described as terminal; there was no cure. My parents were so distraught the doctor had a nurse give them both a tranquilizer.

I remained admitted to the hospital where I began my long running impression of a human "pin-cushion". I encountered so many needles that I got use to them and they were so routine to me, my catch-phrase at the hospital became, "Just tell me when you're gonna stick me!" One of my doctors was so taken by how I always said that, he jokingly commented to my parents that if I ever wrote a book about this, that should be the title. Children's Hospital became my second home.

The doctors presented my parents with the prognosis that I had a 50/50 chance of living five years. This, of course, meant there was a 50% chance of making it to a maximum life expectancy of 10 years old. Every day could theoretically be my last. My parents were then told that some experimental procedures could be tried in an attempt to possibly improve my odds. My desperate parents agreed, and it was decided I would receive 36 days of Neuraxis radiation to all vital organs including my brain and reproductive system as well as a prescribed three years of Chemotherapy.

My mom's repeating chant became, "Why him? Why him?" While repeating this, a nurse who was adjusting my IV came over to my mother, shook her finger at her and said, "You are not even giving him a chance. You are boxing and burying him without giving him a fighting chance!" Then she walked away. When she said that to her, my mom says she thought, "What does she mean I am not giving him a chance?" She said it felt like a slap in the face. "He is in the best hospital in the area, and they tell us these doctors are the best hematologists in the area. What does it mean 'I'm not giving him a fighting chance'?"

On the way home that night she thought about what the nurse had said to her that afternoon. She realized what she was being told was that she had given up on God and wasn't even praying. She went to my bedroom, dropped to her knees at my bedside and cried out to God, "Please God — Please God — Please help my Anthony — please cure him!" She thought of Mary, the mother of Jesus, and how if anyone knew her heart that night, it would be her. How her heart must have ached watching her son die. She cried out again, "Please, please God help me!" Then she crawled up on the bed and cried herself to sleep. She found comfort that night as God felt her heart of desperation.

The next morning my mother awoke feeling refreshed and said she felt a strength she had never experienced before. She knew nothing of it, but she felt the peace and comfort of God's Holy Spirit. She says she just knew that she knew that she knew that I would be ok!

Mom went to my closet and got some of my clothes. Each day she would go to the hospital and dress me in my regular clothes as she stayed with me from early in the morning to late at night, praying and playing with me. Although in the hospital, she wanted me to feel as normal as possible all the while reminding me that God was healing me. She treated me more like I had a cold than incurable cancer. My dad would commute to the hospital twice a day as he continued to work to keep our family business going, and he tended to the needs of my older siblings, Frank and Marie.

My mom was very grateful for the "wake-up call" that nurse had given her and she attempted to find her so that she might thank her. Mom never could find her again and she even described her to the other nurses of that close knit hospital floor, but no one knew of anyone even remotely matching her description. Mom wonders if she had an encounter with an angel.

Mom was experiencing the peace of having yielded her life to Jesus, but Dad had not yet and many times at night she would hear him sobbing when he assumed she was asleep.

I was moved to a private room next to the nurses' station. One wall had huge windows where I could be kept under closer observation. What my mom didn't know at first was that they were not only watching me but they seemed to have seen an obvious change in her demeanor compared to when I was first diagnosed and admitted. On the eighth day one of my hematologists, an intern, and the head nurse came in to talk with my mom.

The doctor asked, "Mrs. Rabak, do you realize the seriousness of your son's illness?"

"YES!" was her reply.

"Do you understand that he has acute lymphoblastic leukemia?"

"YES!" came the reply.

"Do you realize there is a 50/50 chance for his surviving five years?"

"YES!"

"Do you realize there is no cure for leukemia?"

"YES" Mom answered. "But God is going to heal him!"

The doctor said, "I am very happy that you have this faith, but I also want you to be realistic!" To which my mom responded, "With God's help, we will break medical history!"

Later that night my mom wrestled with her thoughts thinking, "What kind of mother are you? You are no longer upset about Anthony's illness and people are noticing it." People would drop by and put their arms around her in sympathy and cry. Mom couldn't even shed a tear as she found herself telling them, "Don't cry. PRAY!"

My mom knew that on that night when she cried out to God in my bedroom, she was given a special gift to walk by faith and not by sight! She knew that God had given her the boldness to proclaim what she had said to the doctor, the intern, and the head nurse. On my tenth day in the hospital I was allowed to go home.

That night after they put me to bed, my dad was on the couch sobbing with mixed feelings. He cried partially because he was happy that I was home but also because he was again faced with the heartache of the reality that I would probably die from the leukemia. My mother again was given boldness to go over and cry with my dad as she proclaimed, "In the name of Jesus, you will have your son." This is what my father needed to hear, and he found comfort in her faith.

Chapter 3

Our Trip to Oakland

—⌘—

A close family friend who was like a relative approached my mom about wanting to take me to a service of an evangelist named Kathryn Kuhlman in Philadelphia, Pennsylvania. She mentioned that she was a lady on television that God had been using to heal people, and she asked if my mom had heard of her. Before I became ill my mom had, indeed, come across her TV program while flipping through stations. She'd see this woman in a long flowing white dress who would stretch out the proclamation, "I beelieeeve in miracles!" Something about her would bother my mom, and she'd quickly turn the channel in frustration. Mom found herself reluctantly promising that she'd watch her on TV that next Sunday.

In the meantime one of the customers from my parents' appliance store, who did not know my 'godmother', left a book at their appliance store for Mom entitled, "I Believe in Miracles" by, none other, than Kathryn Kuhlman. As my mom read that book, tears would roll down her cheeks as she read of people who believed God for a miracle, as she was now, and how they were healed! This helped to strengthen her faith; what some call coincidence, I call providence.

My mom soon was excited to hear that Kathryn Kuhlman would be coming to the Oakland Coliseum not far from their home. Word was that you needed to arrive very early to these meetings if you wanted a seat as thousands of people would show up for the services. So early on July 1st, 1974 my parents and I, along with some friends, set off in our R.V. for the Coliseum. We got there at 9 a.m.; the doors were not set to open until 4 p.m. My dad and the others all took turns waiting in line as thousands arrived, while Mom stayed with me in the motor home until the doors were close to being opened. As my mom brought me out to the line, while those waiting were singing and praying, she noticed how windy it was and began to question herself about us being there. You see, my resistance was very low and the slightest chill usually resulted in me having to be admitted to the hospital with pneumonia, which had happened MANY times before. Mom believes she voiced a silent thought, "I must be crazy!" when she heard someone say, "Don't worry about your child. The Lord is here, and He will protect him!"

Once we finally got into the building, Mom says they were singing beautiful songs she had never heard before; people had their hands raised up in the air, and she heard some speaking in other languages she did not recognize. This was all so overwhelming but at the same time, it was beautiful. Mom realized that instead of listening to what Kathryn Kuhlman was saying, she was distracted looking at all these "strange people". She realized later that she hadn't done much praying because she was trying to adjust to what she was seeing and experiencing.

Mom remembers telling my dad after the meeting that she didn't feel discouraged, but that somehow she felt like she wasn't praying in the right way. As the days went by she noticed there began to be a change in how she was praying. Her prayers were no longer repetitive and ritualistic; she found herself conversing with Jesus on a more intimate, one on one basis. Mom found herself confessing all her sins to Him and "laying all her cards on the table", so to speak. Mom began to feel that Jesus wasn't a distant God somewhere "up there" observing us but that He was here with us every minute as a personal friend.

Chapter 4

"I Want to Go Home"

———∽∽∽———

The time following our trip to Oakland was a very exhausting one for my mom and me. We were going to two medical facilities a day while I was undergoing the experimental 36 days of radiation to my vital organs, including the brain and reproductive system. Compared to how modern treatments are performed, this was very archaic as they would just place me under the radiation machine and flip the switch; nowhere near the more precise science it is today. One of the radiation nurses commented to my mother how unusual a patient I was because usually children around my age would need to be sedated before treatment. Mom says that I acted somehow like I knew this was expected of me in this lifetime. Yet, despite our fatigue, when my mom learned that Kathryn Kuhlman also held regular monthly services at the Shrine Auditorium in Los Angeles, Dad obtained tickets for us and my godmother to go. On August 25th, 1974 we all were at the service.

During that service, Mom remembers Kathryn Kuhlman leading the orchestra for a moment as they sang a song called, "Alleluia." Everyone was standing but because I was resting on my mom's lap, she remained seated. Mom was praying and she began to realize that she was so exhausted and just couldn't do this any longer (she thought she had to do this on her own strength). Mom found herself praying, "God, I can't fight any longer, if you really want Anthony, you can have him. But God, I don't feel you sent him to me late in life (remember, she was almost 40 when I was born) to take him away at an early age. I really believe you sent Anthony for a special purpose; I don't know what that is, but help me be the mother I should to this child so that he can serve you well. If you don't heal him physically today, would you heal us spiritually?" As Mom was praying, she says that she heard a strong wind making a "roaring" sound. Then she heard it again, and upon hearing it a third time, she could tell that whatever this was, it seemed to be directing itself towards us. Mom said she felt like warm oil was being poured on her head. She was overcome with a beautiful feeling of peace as she felt herself going limp in her seat. After the sensation passed, she looked down at me and noticed that I had become like a rag-doll passed out in her lap. I was so still that she thought perhaps I had died. Instinctively Mom checked for a pulse as her friend did the same thing at the exact same time without uttering a word. I was fine; just resting in that same overwhelming feeling of peace that my mother had been experiencing.

From that moment on my mother was never the same again, she began to have a growing hunger to read the Bible, and her faith was now stronger than ever! Mom noticed I was improving. I was no longer ending up in the hospital with a high fever upon exposure to the slightest breeze. It seemed that this experience in that auditorium was a turning point; a welcome respite from all those early morning (2-3 a.m.) trips to the ER with a soaring temperature.

My mom again had made arrangements to go to another Kathryn Kuhlman service in L.A. on Oct. 12, 1974 but first I needed to be seen at the hospital on Oct. 10th for a re-evaluation check-up. I had been having headaches all that prior week and had experienced a loss of appetite. They discovered that the hemoglobin level in my blood had dropped to 8 and that I would need a blood transfusion. This in itself was notable because this would only be my second transfusion since my diagnosis. Normally, children with leukemia required blood transfusions every six to eight weeks. When my mom heard that I would need to be re-admitted into the hospital for the transfusion, she asked the nurse if it could wait until Monday. The nurse inquired why and when my mom said it was because she had plane tickets to go that weekend to Los Angeles for a healing service, the nurse grabbed me and said, "Heavens no! He needs a blood transfusion NOW; his hemoglobin is 8." Mom said, "OK; I just thought I'd ask."

I was immediately admitted to the hospital and approximately three hours later, the doctor approached my mother and said he'd heard she wanted to take me somewhere on Sunday, so Mom explained the situation. He said he would start the blood transfusion immediately and that if all went well, he'd stop by as late as possible on Saturday night and release me from the hospital so that we could leave for L.A. Sunday morning. Mom couldn't ask for more and appreciatively thanked the physician. However, it seems God wanted to teach Mom a valuable lesson about looking to Him for our needs and not anyone else.

I experienced complications from the blood transfusion and had developed a very high temperature when the doctor came to see me late Saturday night. He explained to my parents that as my physician he could not in good conscience release me. Dad agreed with him, but Mom adamantly stated that she had enough faith that she'd wrap me in a blanket, take along some acetaminophen and take me to that healing service. The doctor replied, "Oh no! If his fever got to 105° and you couldn't get him to an emergency room, you would never forgive yourself for the rest of your life if something were to happen to him!" Mom's plans changed as she finally conceded.

The following afternoon my mom experienced something that has happened only once in her life so far. Mom heard an audible voice near her right ear that said, "Bow your head in prayer." Mom looked around that second floor room and saw nothing but empty beds and glass windows. No one else was around, and I was unconscious. Mom says she felt goose bumps forming as she bowed her head to obey the command. When Mom finished praying, I awoke from the coma-like state I was in, looked around and said, "Where am I? I'm hungry. I want to go home!" Mom learned that God can meet you wherever you are; you don't need to go to a specific place to find Him.

From that day on, I've never needed another blood transfusion because of leukemia, and I only had a total of two from April 1974 to October 1974! Mom felt an assurance that I had been healed and continued praising God for it. However, the medical community was skeptical and continued my treatments for leukemia. My parents felt powerless to question the doctors.

Chapter 5

Thank You for this Beautiful Night

———⟨⟨⟨⟨◦⟩⟩⟩⟩———

In October 1976, at the age of 7, I contracted what was then a rare form of pneumonia called pneumocystic pneumonia. Due to the other treatments I was receiving for leukemia, my body's ability to fend off infection was greatly compromised, and this condition affected both of my lungs. This illness hit me harder than everything else I had dealt with to that point with the cancer including the 36 days of intensive radiation, chemotherapy, blood poisoning, countless injections, blood draws, bone marrows, and spinal taps just to mention a few! Mom would stay all day with me at the hospital and when she would read the Bible, it would repeatedly fall open to Psalm 46:10 (NIV), *"Be still and know that I am God."*

They were drawing blood from the arteries in my wrists every 15 minutes to measure the concentration of oxygen in my blood. This type of blood draw was excruciatingly painful, and it repeated four times an hour until someone had the idea to bring in a new machine that would leave a needle in my wrist and automatically draw blood for a reading as needed. Unfortunately, this required that my arms be strapped to two wooden IV boards so that I would not pull out the tubes. Today they can get the same oxygen readings from a small device called a pulse oximeter which is clipped over your index finger tip like a weak clothes pin; no needles necessary! It illuminates the end of your finger with a glowing red light, which always reminds me of the "OOUUCCHH" scene in the movie E.T. the Extra-Terrestrial. One of my frustrated memories was of people coming to visit and bringing me really neat looking toys that I was forced to just sit and stare at because my arms and hands were immobilized! As my condition worsened I was moved from the regular Intensive Care Unit to a special section known as Isolated Intensive Care. Anyone who came in to see me had to wash their hands, wear a face mask, gown, and gloves. On October 23, 1976 one of my doctors was called in from home around midnight because my health had taken a critical turn for the worse. His wife even came in to sit with my family. Someone even contacted my mom because they knew of a psychic healer and wanted permission to ask this psychic to come and see me; she would want to spend half an hour alone with me. Fortunately Mom was given discernment and her response was, "No; if my son is going to die, then his soul will go to God."

The doctor called my parents into his office at the hospital where he reconfirmed to them that my condition had taken a turn for the worse. He assured them he was and would be continuing to do everything humanly possible for me. The doctor even said he had contacted the CDC (Center for Disease Control) in Atlanta, Georgia and was having a special medicine flown in for me; a taxi had been dispatched and was waiting at the airport to transport it to the hospital. Mom told my dad and sister to go home, pray and wait for my brother Frank to come home. He was out and didn't even know what my condition now was. She told them that she and I had a battle to fight and that we were going to win!

The doctor told my mom to go in and "talk with him the way you know how".

Once inside, my mom said that I had so many tubes and machines hooked up to me with lights and beeping that she felt like she was in a spaceship! Slowly as the night progressed I eventually ended up being given 100% oxygen because my lungs were losing the ability to put the proper oxygen concentration into my blood-stream. Next it was expected that organs would begin to fail. My breathing became extremely labored, and my heart rate increased to 185 beats per minute. I was in and out of consciousness and when I was awake, I would beg to have some water; however, they wouldn't give me any because they felt the next move might be that I would need to have an emergency tracheotomy. Because of this, they needed to keep me from ingesting any liquids. There was even an anesthesiologist kept on call for when this might become necessary. My pleas for water became so adamant that to appease me they would dampen a sponge stick and very infrequently touch it quickly and lightly to my lips. It was agony! We so often take the little things for granted!

Mom kept reminding me how much Jesus loved me, and she began to recall a book she had recently read that encouraged praying for a gravely sick person by placing your hand on the person as you tell the devil that as a child of God he has no right to them; so, this is what my mother did. Afterwards she says that I spoke out and thanked the Lord for that beautiful night. I have no recollection of what my mom had said or did but I do remember that evening.

I was laying face up on the hospital bed with my eyes closed, and above me was an examination lamp that was turned on. I could sense the light coming through my closed eyelids. I remember having once been told that in all circumstances (good and bad) we should always thank God even if we don't understand it. I could tell the brightness of the light above me was getting brighter and brighter and I kept my eyes closed as I thought to myself, "Thank you, Lord, for this beautiful night!" Mom says I actually spoke those words out loud. After that I fell into a deep peaceful sleep whereas previously all night I had been delirious and very restless. I was so still, in fact, that Mom thought that perhaps I had died, but the presence of a normal pulse proved otherwise! The next morning I awoke with a hearty appetite and was anxious to go home as if nothing bad had taken place during the night before.

I improved that day, but the doctors were still cautious because they feared what irreparable damage they would find when they investigated what the disease had done to my lungs. There had only been one other leukemia patient at the hospital who had survived this type of pneumonia and their lung was horribly damaged as a result, and here I suffered it in BOTH of my lungs! They didn't expect me to survive, and I think they felt it would have been more humane if I hadn't because I would probably end up permanently on a respirator machine to stay alive. Anyway, x-rays were taken of my lungs to survey the damage and there was something wrong with the films; they seemed over-exposed by a bright light. They said they would have to repeat the films. When the results came back for a second time, they told my parents that the x-rays were so clear it was unbelievable; it was almost as if I had new lungs! Mom remarked to them that this didn't happen because of her but that God wanted them all to see what He could do! Still, the devil wants to discourage us with doubt. After I was home and back at school, one morning my mom was at the church next to my school praying. With a heavy heart she said, "Lord I have faith, but what if…" As she opened her Bible it opened to John 11:4 (NIV), *"This sickness will not end in death. No, it is for God's glory so that God's Son may be glorified through it."* Mom knows that as a result of my two illnesses many have been pointed to God and have come to believe, including my father whom she prayed for six years!

Now you may say, "That's great for you, but I don't believe there is a God, **or** a devil!" That's fine, but it doesn't mean they aren't a reality. It's like someone saying I don't believe in gravity. However, let me take them to the top of the Empire State Building and push them off. Odds are they'll become a believer sometime between the roof of the building and the sidewalk!

You might say, "I won't believe they are real until I can fully understand them; I need to be rational in what I believe in." Ever taken a flight in an airplane? It would seem illogical that a huge, heavy metal tube with wings could take you from point A to point B in the sky, yet thousands get in them everyday without even so much as a second thought about understanding all the principals of physics, aeronautics and aerodynamics. They trusted blindly their first time because they knew of others who had experienced and enjoyed the modern marvel of flight! It might be a new experience, but it's worth it!!

You may not believe in God, but He believes in you!

Chapter 6

Spared for a Purpose

M y parents were told of two possible side-effects from my cancer treatments, which at the time seemed inconsequential, compared to death! One of these was a hindered mental development and, secondly, a shortened stature. I was a short kid and now I'm a short adult (saves my spouse from a sore neck); however, God was gracious to me and I excelled in school. With the leukemia behind me I lived a pretty normal childhood, aside from having a VERY over-protective mother. Can you blame her?

My mom always reminded me while growing up that my life was not my own; she had given me back to God who had spared my life for some special purpose. I had always gone to parochial (Catholic) school so I thought I had a pretty good handle on WHO God was. There is, however, a difference between knowing *about* God and *knowing* God; having a relationship with Him and not religion.

I had no further major medical hurdles for almost ten years, until 1986. I was on a school trip to Washington D.C. when I became very ill with the Epstein-Barr virus, more commonly known as infectious mononucleosis (Mono) or "the kissing disease"; although that certainly wasn't the cause with me! I recovered from that episode and everything was going fine until I encountered an after-effect of my early years. You see, when I was undergoing chemotherapy, my immune system was compromised and normal childhood illnesses presented possibly fatal consequences. One such feared condition that I was kept away from was chicken pox. Whenever a kid at school had the pox, I got a school vacation which I thought was kind of cool. This, however, meant that when I did finally get chicken pox I was 18, and it was a very severe case. It was no fun, but I survived and even have a few scars to remind me of the ordeal.

I grew up in a Christian environment, regularly attending church and I was involved in a youth group. I had all sorts of 'head knowledge' of what it takes to be a Christian; who Jesus Christ is, theology, etc. I'd even experienced a few miracles first hand. Sadly, the distance between one's head and one's heart can seem a million miles apart. I heard that someone once said the greatest trip experienced is about 18 inches, the distance from your head to your heart. Still, despite this expanse, my heart did long to follow God and to discover the purpose for my life that my mother spoke of. I even made some half-hearted altar call decisions to invite God into my life. I convinced myself that the knowledge I had of God was enough to live a Christian life. I even talked a pretty good game; a skill honed while attempting to get my parents to not worry so much about their "baby". I put on a good show on Sundays but did not think too much about God the rest of the week.

One thing I knew from an early age was what I wanted to do with my future. I wanted to be a medical doctor; a pediatrician to be specific. This focus thrilled my parents, and it made my friends envious that I had already decided what I wanted to do with my life. People used to greet me as I was growing up by saying, "What's up, Doc?" I was even convinced that this was God's will for my life, and I said so too! My whole life was centered on this one goal, and my academics reinforced that this was an attainable goal. The fact that it was once said that my mental development might be hindered by some of the cancer treatments I had received further reinforced to me that this must be a part of the plan God had for me.

In 1987 I graduated from high school as the Salutatorian of my class with a 5.0 grade point average (weighted by honors classes) with plans for the fall term of attending the University of California at Davis to continue my journey towards a life in medicine.

Chapter 7

New Freedoms

―❦―

"Your talk talks and your walk talks; But, your walk talks more than your talk talks."

As quoted in the article "Non—
Christians: Friends or Foes?"
From the online newsletter:
Rick Warren's Ministry Toolbox

I set off to college with a lot of anticipation, and I was pleased to find that I would be staying in a dorm "suite" designed to house four students. It consisted of two bedrooms joined by a center common area. I was even more pleasantly surprised to discover that my three roommates were all going to be friends of mine from high school, this added to my excitement! The four of us were like "kids in a candy store" enjoying the new found freedoms of having no one to impose curfews on us or tell us where to go and not to go. What we were quick to discover was that with this freedom also came responsibility.

One such place that my roommates and I should not have gone was to a fraternity house party where I threw caution to the wind and when someone put a beer in my hand, I drank it. When a refill came, I drank it too, and the one after it and so on. The next morning I was at a porcelain altar presenting my offering! When my friends saw how funny I was when drunk, they decided later to have a party in our room and get me drunk so those in my dorm could enjoy what a cut-up I was when intoxicated. I was popular but for the wrong reasons.

My roommates and I looked forward to the time when our first set of college grades would come; after all we were all high school honor students and expected to academically conquer college the same way we had conquered high school. As we each opened our reports we were astonished to discover a common thread; we were all placed on academic probation due to poor academic performance. We all felt there had to be some sort of mix up at the Registrar's office; these could not possibly have been our grades, especially when you were to consider our positive track records in high school.

Plus, our names were not on these reports, only student ID numbers and we mistakenly thought that maybe they were not ours.

Well, no mistakes had been made. The fault was our own for not taking our studies seriously. We were too busy goofing off and enjoying our "freedom" to study! If our grades did not improve significantly in the near future and remain up, we could be expelled from the University. I was horrified because I knew my future career was in danger. I immediately pulled in the reigns and dedicated myself to my studies and the grades came up accordingly; however, I needed to maintain them. The tension of this new academic focus caused me to not be as easy going as I had been in the previous months. I began to have a short fuse with my room-mates who were also working hard to get their grades up. The difference was that they were maintaining their sense of humor, at least at first. Our dorm room was small and we always seemed to be under each others' feet or in some way being a disturbance to each other. I see it this way: if you take sibling rats and keep them together in a small cage as they grow, they will eventually turn on each other. Our living situation eventually became very tense; and as they say, familiarity began to breed contempt.

I think one of the worst things I've ever done is described in the Bible in Titus 1:16. I professed God with my mouth, yet denied Him with my deeds. As I said, when I went away to college my roommates were friends of mine from my high school. These guys saw my life on an everyday but Sunday basis; the good, the bad, and unfortunately, the ugly. People at church saw Anthony, the Sunday angel; these guys saw the weekday devil. Don't get me wrong; I wasn't horrible, I just thought about God at church and myself through the week. I always professed to be a Christian, but my lifestyle didn't always show it. Actions do speak louder than words.

One day I heard about a Christian student group that met on the campus and being a "Christian" myself, I thought I'd check them out. I quickly made friends with one of the leaders of the group and one day he came to my dorm room for a visit. I introduced him to one of my roommates, and they began to have a deep conversation. Before long, he began to share about how great it was to have a personal relationship with Jesus, how if you accept Him as your savior He can transform your life for the better if you let Him. He ended his statements by saying, "...just like he's done in Anthony's life!" I could see the confused look come across my roommate's face as he stated that my life didn't seem any different from his. Suddenly the reality set in that my playing games with God was impacting the salvation of another person's soul, and not positively.

When my "visitor" left, I hung my head in shame and apologized to my roommate. I told him everything that had just been shared with him was indeed correct and that I was guilty of forgetting those truths. I admitted that I had been showing a horrible example of what a committed Christian should be. I don't know where he is today, but I pray that better reflections of Christ have crossed his path and hopefully undone the damage that I did. More is done to hurt Christianity by the *vocal deceived* than the *silent saints*. I saw it written once that "The BEST sermon is a GOOD example". What a true statement that is!

I am reminded of a time later on in my life when I met an older man who came up to me after a meeting where I was sharing my testimony. He gingerly walked up to me, aided by his wife who was holding his arm. It was quite obvious that he was suffering from paralysis on one side of his body. He spoke no words as tears were violently streaming done his face. His wife spoke for him as he had tremendous difficulty talking. It seemed that he had been a successful, long time pastor who had recently suffered a stroke. His wife shared how he used to love preaching about God, how he had been a gifted speaker. He now felt robbed of his calling, his voice and his composure and he stood before me now broken, feeling that he was no longer of any earthly good to God. I didn't know how to respond. I just felt led to take his hands, bow my head and begin to pray. God began to speak to this elderly saint as He led my words and my praying. I don't remember exactly what I said but it alluded to the fact of how pleased God was in his life of ministry to others and that as he faced this present hardship with an unfaltering faith in Jesus Christ, he would now be preaching the greatest sermon of his life without uttering a word. Great would be his reward. I am humbled that God would allow me the privilege to share His words of encouragement with a man who was so loved by Him and as I write these words it strengthens me in my journey. I pray that God will be glorified in the silence of my life; in my actions more than my words.

Chapter 8

Shattered Pieces

———∽∾∽———

Back at college my sister came to visit me that first part of the school year. Things were going well with our visit and then she brought up the dreaded topic of how my grades were doing. I didn't want to lie to her and told her of my recent episode of being on academic probation. She didn't take it so well and told me I better shape up or she'd tell Mom & Dad and I'd probably get sent back home to go to community college. I know she wasn't trying to hurt me; I know how much she loves me. Her intention was only to provide me with the necessary "incentive" to straighten up and fly right. What ended up happening was an excessive fear that loomed over me because I mistakenly assumed that a medical school would not accept a student who had gone to a community college.

Then another unexpected surprise came; a high school girlfriend called me and we fought over the phone, ultimately ending our relationship. She stated that I was no longer the person I used to be, even throwing in a statement that I used to be concerned about God and that I no longer seemed to be. I felt that this was some kind of a petty excuse for the breakup she seemed to want.

I began to survey the recent events of my life and they began to overwhelm me like an avalanche: academic probation, strained relationships and tension with my roommates, the threat of my parents finding out about my slacking off and the fear of going to a community college, the girlfriend breakup; the pressure began to intensely build. I decided I'd do what always helped before when I experienced stress and needed to vent, which was to take my hot-rod out for a drive. The next sequence of events is detailed in the Prologue. If you have not yet read it, now is the time. If you have, please re-read it for a refresher; then meet me back here.

— —

I was headed the wrong way! Instead of taking eastbound Highway 80 towards Reno, I was headed in the westbound direction towards my hometown in the East

Bay Area. As soon as I realized my directional error I determined to take the next freeway off ramp to alter my direction. Then the soundtrack started up again stating how things were really messed up and that there was no way for me to handle this; however, I knew somehow in my heart that this time something was different; the statement was coming from God.

God?! I could accept messages of discouragement coming from the devil, but why would a seemingly hopeless message like this be coming from God? The problem was that my own thoughts were interrupting Him, and when I finished interjecting, the rest of the message came through loud and clear. I had really screwed things up this time, and I was correct that there was no way I could handle this on my own. BUT, if I would give this situation to Him, He would help me. God wants to piece back together the shattered remnants of a broken life. He just waits on us. God patiently waits until we realize the futility of trying to live life without Him; until we realize our need for Him. For the first time that night I felt hope, not condemnation.

Ok God, you have my rapt attention…

I began to think about that image of the broken picture window that represented my life, all of the countless shattered pieces and how on my own I could not repair this damage. God, however, can make the impossible

possible. I felt encouraged to give Him *all* of the pieces and He would restore it, the missing key of previous attempts in my life. The missing ingredient was to give God ALL of the pieces. I had at times before thought I'd give God a try, but I always gave Him all the messed up and broken pieces of my life and held on to those areas which I thought I could handle on my own. The funny thing is that these ended up being the areas where future problems would originate. God encouraged me that if I give Him <u>ALL</u> of the pieces He would not stop at just repairing the window; He'd replace the whole pane of glass! Consider this; would you be satisfied looking at a beautiful view through a patched up window, one in which the broken pieces had merely been taped or glued back together? Such a window would be functional, but it wouldn't be much to look at — or through! The key being not to give God only 98% or even 99% of your life but a total and complete 100%.

I determined what the next course of action needed to be; to give my life in it's entirety over to God's control. I kept on my present course and decided that I'd go see the youth minister at my church back home. However, I was suddenly struck with the admonition that I should not go see this person but that I should go see my dad. I know this was God's prompting because my parents were the last people that I would choose to go see to admit how my life was not right and that I needed help. You see, I thought I had them convinced that I had my act together. I did find it very odd that I was being encouraged to not go to see my youth pastor; I thought he'd be the perfect person for this job, and my parents wouldn't even need to know. Again the urging came, DON'T go to my youth pastor, DO go see my dad. As I drove, I volleyed my thoughts on this issue back and forth against God's prompting like a professional ping pong match. Remember when I referenced the "time warp driving phenomenon"? Well, I continued to debate the issue with God and before I knew it, I was setting the parking brake on my car in the driveway of my parents' house!

It was now quite late at night and no one was expecting me, so when I rang the bell I was given a long inquisition from the other side of the door by my startled mother. I asked her to please open the door and wake Dad so I could talk with him. Without going into a lot of details I told them how I had come to realize that I had been playing around in my relationship with God and that I needed to dedicate 100% of my life to Him. What came next from them floored me.

"Is this about your drug problem?"

"What?!" I asked

"It's ok; your youth pastor already told us that you were having a problem with drugs."

I told them that I had previously gotten drunk at a party or two at school and that I had tried marijuana twice in the past but had stopped. I assured them I did not have a drug "problem". I had just come to the realization that my life needed to be completely yielded to Jesus, so with my dad leading me, this is exactly what took place that night. It felt like a heavy weight had lifted off my shoulders, and the feelings of hopelessness and condemnation were nowhere to be found. I felt HOPE; tomorrow would be a new day!

I did wonder where that youth pastor had gotten the idea that I was having a problem with drugs, and then it dawned on me. I remembered that one weekend evening I was back near my hometown getting fuel for my Camaro at a local gas station. As I was pumping my gas, a car pulling a moving trailer pulled up to me and the driver said he was new to the area and that he got the word on the street that I could help him score, that he heard that I was the "dope-man". Confused, I told him that he had the wrong guy. Then it clicked; another guy in town had a very dark green 1969 Camaro with white racing stripes and at night it was very easy to confuse my black 1968 Camaro with white racing stripes for his. Friends later told me that HE was the individual with a reputation for dealing drugs. My youth minister must have heard the rumor and mixed me up with him. I never learned why he chose to go to my parents with this information instead of speaking directly with me. I had approached my folks first before they had figured out how to approach the subject with me. This "pastor" had already left the ministry and the area before I was able to find an answer. I hope others can learn from his mistake; I sure did!

I went home for the Christmas break in 1987 and while in town, I went out one evening with a friend I had gone to high school with who was also home for the holidays. As we discussed what had taken place since graduation, he began to explain all the difficulties he was having during his first year away at the college he was attending in Southern California. His problems were very much like what I had been experiencing so I shared with him what I had recently done in fully yielding my life to God. I explained to him the peace I was now experiencing because of that decision and I led him in giving control of his heart to God too. Later that night as I walked with him out to his car I began to sense that there was something he wanted to get off his chest. When I probed further and assured him he could share anything with me, he dropped the bombshell. It turned out to be that he had been seeing my ex-girlfriend and it started before we had even broken up. Immediately

I began to sense my fist tighten up and I think he fully anticipated me to try and take a swing at him, although I wasn't much of a fighter. I was able to restrain myself as I realized how I would be throwing away everything I had said to him earlier about God changing my heart. I released the tension in my fist and found myself telling him that I forgave him. He told me how he knew that what I had said earlier was real because that was not at all what he had expected; truthfully, neither did I. I realized now why my girlfriend had ended our relationship. With this very much unexpected response, I knew too that God had indeed changed my heart!

Chapter 9

Ducks in a Row

———◈———

The day after I gave my life to God completely felt like a dream. Somehow the sky seemed bluer, the grass was greener and each individual blade seemed backlit by tiny spotlights. The birds sang louder and more melodious, the flowers were all so vivid and bold; a stark contrast from the blandness of the previous day. I've heard the saying, "What a difference a day makes", but I would add "with Jesus!" He changes your perspective.

In the days that followed I took a walk in the Arboretum, a beautiful place on the university campus created to be a place for the students to relax with the serenity of nature, away from the pressures of school. As I walked around the small pond I saw a mother duck come out from behind a bush. Following her were about eight ducklings all in a single file line. Every turn she made as she walked was mirrored by the baby ducklings. If she turned left, they turned left. When she turned right, they turned right. They continued doing this all the way down to the water's edge. As she jumped in, they followed suit remaining in that perfect line while they swam. As I watched this, God began to speak to my heart.

If I were given the task, to take those little ducks and put them in a single file line, could I do it? Seems simple enough in theory, but in reality it would be impossible for me to do. I might get the first couple of ducks and set them in a line one behind the other, but as I would go for the third duck the first would most likely wander off, and as I placed #1 back and went for #3, then #2 would meander, and so forth. Remember there are eight of them; a true lesson in futility! God was showing me something; if I trusted Him with all the various details and aspects of my life, He had the authority over those things and would handle them for me. He would make the details of my life line up. He would make sure all my "ducks were in a row". The key was to make sure He had complete and total control of them all. Wow, I was blown away by this reality.

I was so excited that my life had new hope, and I was grateful because I knew that it was because of God.

I knew that I desired to dedicate myself to serving Him, but I always felt that the way I would do this was by serving mankind as a physician. I knew that it was going to be a long road yet before this would be accomplished, my heart was so grateful I wanted to do something to serve Him sooner. A thought entered my mind one day as I read about an extra-curricular course that was being offered at the university to get training as an EMT, an Emergency Medical Technician. That was it! I could get a part-time job working on an ambulance crew while going to school and this would be a way to serve God in the medical field now while getting myself acquainted working with patients, hospitals, nurses and doctors; a WIN-WIN-WIN-WIN situation!

I prayed and asked God to not let me waste my time, to close the door if this was something that I should not pursue. I felt alright about going forward, so I anxiously signed up for this night course. At the first class I realized that this would be a considerable time commitment and because I had a full course load during the day, I felt I'd better have a talk with the class instructors. I told them that I was concerned because I did not have an exemplary driving record due to my high school days with a muscle-car, and I did not want to continue with the class if it would be a hindrance to me getting a job as an EMT. They asked if I had any DUI's; I did not. Any reckless driving citations? I did not. "Then what?"

they asked. Well, a few speeding tickets, some infractions for failure to come to a complete stop (rolling, or 'Hollywood Stops') and I once ran a stoplight. I was asked with a laugh, "What do you think you'll be doing most of the time as an ambulance driver? Consider it practice!" They told me there was a shortage of EMTs and that I should have no problem finding a job.

It was a busy schedule but I was managing it, and at the end one final detail remained that needed to be done to complete the course. I would need to have a routine physical exam so the DMV would issue the special license needed to drive an ambulance. Some friends told me that you could get a free check up at the student health clinic on campus. I made the appointment then set the rest of the afternoon aside to inquire about jobs at local ambulance companies. Things were going well at the first stop until they asked to see a copy of my driving record; they turned me down. I shrugged it off and went to the next service on my list. Everything was going fine there too, until they asked for my driving record; turned away again! The story was the same at each company I visited. They wanted to hire me but knew they'd be restricted from doing so because of my driving record. Seems their insurance companies would not allow me to drive their expensive ambulances. I tried to plead with them, promising that I would not drive but only be a medical tech in the back of the rig. They all said that this was not possible as the job required each crew member to trade off and share the driving responsibility equally. This was not negotiable!

I harbored resentment toward God, as I felt He had allowed my time to be wasted. I remembered praying specifically for the doors of opportunity with the EMT class to be closed if I was not to pursue this. Downhearted I figured I had come this far, I might as well keep the appointment for the physical, get my license and certification, and then maybe in a year or two when my driving record purged some of my offenses then I might be able to get hired. I might as well try.

The day came for the physical, and it seemed to go pretty quickly. The doctor was nearing the completion of the exam and was finishing writing some chart notes when suddenly he stopped, turned around and came back to examining me. As he was feeling my neck he asked if I had recently been sick or if I felt like I might be coming down with a cold. I told him that I was feeling fine. Feeling a slight lump in my neck he asked if I would be willing to have it looked at further. He stated that it probably wasn't anything to be too concerned about but that it should be checked out because of my extensive medical history and the extent of the radiation I had received while undergoing treatment for leukemia. An appointment was made for a needle aspiration to have the small mass tested.

Had I known what was involved in the procedure, I'm not sure that I would have been so quick in agreeing! I soon found myself lying on a table as they prepared to stick a large needle into the front of my neck to obtain a biopsy sample. I'm not sure what hurt more, the needle or the test results! It was determined that I had papillary thyroid cancer, a side effect from my childhood radiation treatments. The results felt about as exciting as a good, swift kick in the stomach! How could this be? I had recently surrendered my future into God's hands and this is what I get? Not only did I feel that He had let me down by allowing my efforts and time to be wasted by taking the EMT course, but now I had cancer... again!

If there was one thing I recalled from my studies in Catholic school it was the admonition that you had better not cause another to stumble in their walk with God (Mark 9:42 & Luke 17:2). So I put on a happy face and professed to others that I was going to trust God for the outcome in this. If God could see me through leukemia, He could surely see me through this. The truth was, I said the words aloud but inside I felt too hurt to fully believe what I professed. Fortunately, God looks at the heart and deep inside me there was still a mustard seed sized amount of faith there.

The time came for me to go into the hospital for what was supposed to be a one and a half hour operation. The 90 minutes passed and by the time I was taken to recovery, seven and a half hours had elapsed. When I finally awoke from anesthesia, the doctors told me what they had encountered. Seems the cancer had spread outside of the thyroid gland and into the surrounding lymph nodes. They removed the nodes one at a time and sent them for testing, and they had to keep me "under" while they waited for the lab results to come back to indicate that all of the cancer had been removed. They said the cancer had spread extensively up my neck but that it had only gone down as far as my clavicle bone; it stopped just short of dropping down into my chest cavity. They said that this cancer was slow growing and had been there for some time. They said that I must have had an excellent specialist who caught this at the perfect time. If any more time had lapsed and the cancer had made it down into my chest, then it would most likely have spread and they would have had a much harder time removing it, if at all. The scope of this didn't sink in... yet.

I remember being in tremendous pain. You're not quite aware of just how many muscles are involved in the task of supporting and turning your head until you've had one removed and the rest poked, prodded, and stretched to their limits by a thyroidectomy with some lymph node resections thrown in for good measure. Trust me; we take them for granted! The only way I found to sit up in bed was to grab the front of my hair and pull forward and up; NOT fun.

Needless to say, this whole situation did nothing to further my endearment to God. I felt He was somehow to blame for my present situation.

Chapter 10

Blame

A s I sat in the hospital room, my head was swimming in a vortex of confusion and anger. What was the use? Why live your life following after God? I was always told that if you follow God and do what is right that it would be something positive in your life. Well, I was finding just the opposite happening; whenever I tried to live for God, bad things happened. I was discouraged trying to be a "Christian". It seemed that when I lived my own life and did what I wanted, things sometimes went wrong but they didn't seem as bad as when I tried to live for Him. In my frustration I threw up an ultimatum, "God, I'll leave You alone; You leave me alone! Let's try that for a while." Feeling some satisfaction that I had spoke my mind, shaking a clay fist at the Potter, I closed my eyes and tried to get some rest.

There was a ventilation duct above my bed; from it emanated a low, soft sound that I focused on as I tried to relax my mind. As I was drifting off in that gray area between consciousness and sleep, something disturbing began to happen. The low, droning sound in that ventilation duct began to increase in volume, and the soothing monotone sound behind the grate began to fluctuate, sounding kind of like the soundtrack from a horror movie depicting human souls in Hell; voices in torment. The room seemed to darken, and the hair on the back of my neck began to stand on end as I began to feel a presence of evil in the room. I tried to open my eyes to see what was going on but I couldn't open them. My heart began to race. I tried to move, and my body felt paralyzed. Now I was really beginning to panic!

Ironically, I instinctively remembered being taught as a child that if I ever felt in danger to say the name "Jesus" because there was power in His name. This is what I decided to do (remember, this is the same person who moments before had told God to leave him alone). I tried to open my mouth and say the name of Jesus, but nothing came out. I struggled and tried again but I physically began to feel heaviness on my chest and I couldn't catch my breath. The best way I can describe what I felt was that I had a sensation like someone was sitting on my chest and cupping my mouth to prevent me from speaking. I struggled with all my might and whimpered out the name, but absolutely nothing happened. I tried to fight this overwhelming sensation but it seemed to grow more intense the harder I fought to move, speak, or breathe. Suddenly a thought came to me that perhaps this is what it feels like when you are dying and that I shouldn't fight against this. I loosened my struggle and thought I'd just let it happen. After a half-hearted sigh, I tried to relax my body and wait for this new experience to overtake me.

What happened next caught me by surprise. I clearly heard this admonition in my mind, "Do NOT use My Son's name unless you mean it!" It suddenly dawned on me that I was merely trying to say Jesus' name not because I was honestly seeking His rescue but because I was just trying to escape this "situation". Repentantly, my inner self cried out to God apologetically, then the name began to form on my lips and my spirit cried out in a loud, forceful voice; it actually kind of startled me, "JESUS!!" Immediately, like snapping out of a nightmare, the room returned to normal, the heaviness on my chest was gone, I gasped but breathed deeply without effort, my eyes opened to the brightness of the room, I was again able to move, and the register above my bed was churning out the low, monotonous, yet soothing sound of the ventilation system. Gone was the feeling of evil, and I felt only a tremendous sense of relief that this episode was over. Repeatedly, between almost hyper-ventilating breaths, words of gratitude and praise to God were on my lips. I told God that if I ever uttered something stupid like asking Him to leave me alone again, to please disregard my request.

Upon contemplating what happened I became aware of this fact — God truly loves us all and wants to draw us into a right relationship with Him. Because of that tremendous, unselfish love He affords us a certain degree of protection over our lives while He is being revealed to us, regardless of our status with Him. The Bible states in Romans 5:8 (NIV)..."While we were still sinners, Christ died for us." God is a gentleman, and if we specifically instruct Him to remove Himself from our lives, He will reluctantly comply. This was my grave error when I told Him to leave me alone, yet even in this it only served to reinforce my desperate need for Him, and He was graciously awaiting my repentant cry. I remember in Bible school having a discussion with classmates on what Hell is like. There were, of course, many beliefs but there was one common thread: Hell is a place of absence from the presence of God. In this experience I feel that God allowed me a very small sliver of the taste of what Hell is like without His presence; it is not something that I would wish on my worst enemy, and I pray that none of you will ever experience it!

I spent the remainder of that night gratefully focused on God, and He began to enlighten my understanding of a few things, things that sustain me even to this day.

Chapter 11

The Battlefield

———◁୬୬▷———

S atan did a good job in getting me to believe that every bad thing that happened to me was somehow directly linked back to God. If something went wrong, I blamed Him. Well that night in the hospital while recovering from my thyroid cancer operation, God allowed me to see the truth. He loves me and wants only the best for me just like it states in Jeremiah 29:11 (NIV), *"For I know the plans I have for you," declares the LORD, "plans to prosper you and not to harm you, plans to give you hope and a future."* To allow me to better understand why things happen the way they sometimes do, He gave me the following example:

Picture this world and your life as a battlefield with a line of neutrality separating it in half, with God as the

General on one side and where Satan has established himself as a general on the other. The Devil has as his "troops" under him, the fallen angels and demons, his principalities and powers (Ephesians 6:12), then closer to the line of neutrality are those who willingly choose to follow him. Closer yet to the line are those who choose to live for themselves and don't even think about God or the devil. In not choosing a side, they inadvertently have.

Matthew 12:30 (MSG) says, "This is war, and there is no neutral ground. If you're not on My side, you're the enemy; if you're not helping, you're making things worse."

Now, on God's side He has the Angels and those of mankind that have chosen to follow Him. Just as there are varying ranks in a worldly army, so there is too among Christians. Closest to that line of neutrality are the Christians who have accepted Jesus in their heart but they do nothing further. They want to be on the winning side and believe in having "fire insurance" against going to hell, but that's the extent of it. It's kind of like those who were drafted into the army; they fear being counted as "Absent Without Leave", or "AWOL". They're content to remain ducked down in a foxhole or on kitchen patrol (KP). They'd rather clean latrines than be on the front lines. Next in the ranks are those who enlist voluntarily but, too often, for ulterior motives.

They've joined to get, not give — like those who join under the G.I. Bill — they want money for college or to learn a new skill for a future career; they never signed up expecting to see active combat and when called upon they reluctantly serve and do the bare minimums. Next are those who thrill God's heart; Christians who are like officers or even higher — they eat, breathe, and sleep the ARMY — they have chosen to make it a career. The army is the first thing on their mind when they wake up, it's also the last thing on their mind when their head hits the pillow at night. They may not have started out on this journey gung-ho, maybe as enlisted personnel or even as drafted soldiers, but they have caught the vision and moved up in the ranks to be where God wants all Christians to be.

Then God told me to picture myself in the enemy's shoes; who would pose the greater risk to me? The drafted? No, they can be kept in the kitchen, latrine, or ducked down in foxholes pretty easily without expending too much energy. How about the enlisted? They require a little more weaponry, but not a lot. Officers and the higher ranks? They're the ones who require more artillery; they don't discourage as easily. That's where the big guns have to be unleashed.

God's warfare works the opposite from the world's. We are more of a threat to the enemy not by rushing over the line towards our adversary but by retreating from the line and drawing closer to God, our General and Father. The very situations that the devil intends to cause us to withdraw or rebel from God should now serve as the catalyst to cause us to run to Him and not from Him. Now it made sense! The light had been turned on. Whenever I made a conscious decision to know God more and desired His plans for my life, that's when I would become more of a threat to the enemy and he would "turn up the heat" to try and discourage me, causing me to mistakenly blame God for any misfortune I experienced. It all made sense now!

Now that I know who's truly to blame, I can fully put my trust in God and say, "Satan, bring it on!" With God, I'll only come out better than before! In these seasons of trial, the enemy becomes God's tool. When I allow God to have total control of my hardships, I know that He takes everything the devil intends for evil and turns it around for my good and His glory!

That same night God also gave me another example to see how our trials and tribulations can serve to make us better. Gold refined by fire.

Let's say you're walking along a trail, leisurely kicking rocks as you stride. On one particular kick you uncover a rock with a certain glimmer to it. Upon closer investigation, you notice the source of the shimmer. It appears to be gold, but it's mixed in with other elements in the rock. You could take your discovery down to the mall to see if a jewelry store would put it into a display case with a high price tag to sell alongside the pieces of gold jewelry in their inventory. After all, you think, it has to have some inherent value simply because it has gold in it, right? "Don't hold your breath waiting for a sale", they'll probably tell you. If you want a quicker sale for a commanding price you'll need to take this ore sample to a refiner. They'll separate the gold from the other impurities and purify it. This refining is not done in a single step but is a process of subjecting the sample to varying temperatures, usually by fire. You see, each impurity will respond and either separate or burn off at a different stage or degree. The end results are that the gold purifies a little bit more each time. The higher the karat number, the purer the gold –- 10k, 14k, 18k, 22k, up to what is usually denoted as the commercially purest 24k. Once the gold is refined, then a craftsman can shape it into an attractive piece of jewelry worth more than its mere gold content. When the Devil tries to knock us down with opposition, we have a unique opportunity to give the situation over to God and allow Him to use it as a refining and fashioning time to improve us. What a privilege!

Years later I came across 1 Peter 1:6-7 (NLT) "So be truly glad. There is wonderful joy ahead, even though you have to endure many trials for a little while. These trials will show that your faith is genuine. It is being tested as fire tests and purifies gold — though your faith is far more precious than mere gold. So when your faith remains strong through many trials, it will bring you much praise and glory and honor on the day when Jesus Christ is revealed to the whole world."

Chapter 12

Back to College: Loss of Direction

—◊◊◊—

Having come through this recent trial, I went back to school in 1988 with a renewed sense of focus; look out world — here I come! I felt that things in my life were now going positively. I had given control of my life to God and felt things would now begin to take a more positive shape for me. I didn't have all the answers concerning my life, but I was beginning to gain a better appreciation for what it says in Jeremiah 29:11— God has only good thoughts and plans for us to give us a future and a hope. He works all things out for our good if we will only love and trust in Him.

Remember the doctor at the university free health clinic, the one who uncovered my thyroid cancer? Well,

I usually went home from school on the weekends to attend the church I had gone to as a teenager. I was a peer leader in the youth group there. On one particular weekend not long after that episode, I didn't feel like going home so I stayed in my college town. I had seen a commercial on TV advertising a local church. I decided to go there that weekend and after the service on the way out I saw someone who kind of looked familiar to me. When our eyes met, I realized it was the doctor from the free clinic. When I walked over to shake his hand, he asked how things were after I went to see the specialist he referred me to. After I told him, he shared with me how he prays daily for Jesus to use him and help him be the best physician he can be.

I asked him how long he had been working at the free clinic. He told me that he actually had his own medical practice and that he just donated his time there once a week. His one day a week just happened to be a time when my appointment was. I had a flash back to when I was in the hospital recovering from my thyroid operation and I remembered being told that I must have had an excellent specialist who caught the cancer at the perfect time before it dropped into my chest cavity and possibly metastasized to other parts of my body. I also remembered how I had been mad at God for wasting my time in allowing me to take that EMT course – *the whole reason I needed that DMV physical in the first place!* Coincidence? I believe not! I once heard it explained like this by the character Tess on the old TV show 'Touched by An Angel': "There is no such thing as coincidence; just times when God chooses to remain anonymous!" Look at "coincidences" closely enough and you can usually find God's fingerprints all over the situation.

I continued on with my studies and excelled academically in all of my general education classes. Here is where the roadblock came: if I took a class that was geared toward my future plans of a career in medicine I got mediocre or failing marks. What?! I never suffered with any science, physics, chemistry, or biology classes in high school. "What's going on?" I thought to myself. I re-adjusted my thinking cap and refocused myself, but still there were no improvements. Next step, I humbled myself and went to the student help center and inquired about tutoring. They did some investigation and tests, concluding that I didn't just need tutoring; they felt I may have a learning "disability" and because of this suspicion I would be given extra time when taking an exam. Personally, I thought they were the ones with the learning problem: how could an honor roll high school student have a learning disability? How come I never needed help before? However, I was desperate and when I heard I'd be given time and a half for test taking I said ok, I must have a learning disability (after all, I'm no dummy!). Well, even with the extra test taking time, I still did no better. Oddly, my difficulties were only with classes that would have a direct impact on getting into medical school.

I was devastated, and then it hit me –– was God giving me an indication that maybe He had something else in store for my future? That couldn't be! I KNEW medicine was His plan for me, and I'd known it since I was a kid. The funny thing is that I never bothered to ask His opinion before.

I had a heart to heart with God in my prayers and I told Him that I was tired of what was happening; that if He had other plans for me He would need to remove the intense desire that was in my heart to be a physician. I felt that this didn't seem possible; it had been there since I was a child. I was always very determined and convinced that this was my calling; remember, I was the envy of those friends in high school who had no clue as to what future paths to take. I was "the man with a plan". Turns out I was actually being like a plow horse that needs blinders on so it won't be easily distracted. I had become so focused to the point of exclusion that I wasn't seeing when God was patiently trying to get my attention to show me what His intentions were for my future. I had placed Him on the sidelines and when I noticed something in my peripheral vision (which turned out to be His gentle promptings), I would disregard them as a distraction or something that might divert my attention from pursuing God's plan for me. That's ironic isn't it? I had a lesson to learn; that if I was given too much information at once I would tend to get ahead of myself while trusting my own way instead of His. Seems I can only handle enough grace for a day.

Then it happened; I had been so busy focusing my attention toward overcoming my "learning disability" that I didn't notice what was happening. I began to subconsciously entertain the idea of actually going into something other than medicine. When I stopped to evaluate this, I realized what had happened; my intense desire to become a doctor was undeniably waning.

As I analyzed this further it became so clear to me that as a sick child, my whole life had revolved around medicine; hospitals, clinics, nurses, and doctors! My childhood association of helping people came from physicians and my underlying desire was only to help people; this is what I really wanted. It's logical that I would make such an association –- to me, a way of helping mankind meant to be in medicine (not too bad for a guy with a learning disability, eh?)

OK, I realized this new dynamic. Now what?

Chapter 13

Studies Suspended

—◦◦◦—

During my third year of study at U.C. Davis in 1990, one thing became very clear to me; I was entering the phase of my education where things would begin a major shift from general education classes to focus more on classes pertinent to my major field of study; which in this case was physiology (my pre-medical Major). If medicine was not going to be my future career, now was the time for a change of Major. I had determined that God had other plans for me besides medicine; what that was still eluded me. So that I would not be wasting my efforts, or my parents' money, I felt that I had better take time off from school temporarily until I had a clearer direction.

I suspended my studies and began to focus my attention on other possible career paths. This endeavor was about as clear as mud! My dad kept trying to help me by suggesting possible career choices, and nothing ever even remotely appealed to me. One day he stated how much I seemed to enjoy being a peer leader with the youth group at my church and had I ever considered going into youth ministry? Strangely, the prospect didn't get shut down immediately when it was suggested, but as I thought about it more I convinced myself what this wasn't viable. I assumed that to go into youth ministry one would need to go to a Bible college and the only semi-local one I was familiar with was in Santa Cruz about four and a half hours from Davis. I was not open to relocating. In addition, I knew of no older youth pastors and most regarded youth ministry not as a career but as being a "stepping-stone" to becoming a church senior pastor. I had no desire to do that.

One day I attended a training meeting with my father for a Christian businessman's fellowship he was involved with, and this is where I met someone who would play a part in God changing my life direction. This meeting was in a city about one and a half hours west from where I was currently living in Davis, California. At this gathering I met a man who was an administrative pastor at a large church about 40 minutes east of Davis. When he learned that I was not too far from where he worked, it was suggested by him that we meet to have lunch one day and get to know each other better; sounded good to me, plus I wasn't prone to turning down an offer to have a meal. Well, one day I got a phone call from the church's secretary to facilitate this lunch, and our meeting was on the calendar.

The morning of our meeting came and that same secretary called because something unexpected had come up, our lunch meeting would need to be postponed. I understood that these things happen. The morning came for our rescheduled lunch, and again I received a phone call from the secretary that the meeting would need to be put off. I was polite, but inside I was a little bothered; I always did my best to make it a priority to keep planned commitments.

Well, the morning arrived again for the re-rescheduled lunch and I half prepared myself to receive another call. However, it never came and I found myself in the church office reception area to meet with this gentleman. As I sat waiting, I remembered my dad mentioning that he thought he had heard somewhere that this church had a small Bible college program and that I should inquire about it when I had this meeting. I kept reminding myself to do this when we were face to face. The church secretary told me to go ahead and go into the back to this pastor's office. As I walked in, he stood to shake my hand and said, "Here, I'm supposed to give you this", as he threw a pamphlet down on the desk. It was an informational course catalog for Capital Bible Institute, the small Bible college at this church. I wondered if he had recent communications with my father. "No", was the reply. I asked him why he was giving this to me, and he stated that he wasn't really sure. He said he just had the feeling while praying that morning that this was what he was to do.

Needless to say, we had quite a conversation at lunch! I shared with him how I was kind of idling for the time being. I knew that my life was being led in a new direction but that I was unsure of where to go next. This person told me how he had a similar experience; he was convinced that his direction in life was to go into law enforcement or criminal justice. The time came when he got serious about God and began to yield his life to Him. Floundering, he drew closer to God and focused on deepening a relationship with his Creator and this was when his life course changed. Drawing on why he felt impressed to give me the school catalogue, he said that he never had heard of anyone whose future career paths were hindered by going to Bible school for a year. He suggested that I pray and see if I felt led to dedicate a year to deepening my relationship with God in this way. Perhaps that would help me to gain the clarity I sought. I agreed to consider and pray about it; I did, and shortly thereafter enrolled for the next upcoming year at the Bible school.

In the latter part of 1989, during this "transition" time, I began to have intermittent strange sensations in the lower half of my left hand. It was sort of a combination of numbness and tingling. For reference, if you were to draw a line from the wrist up your middle finger, it was from that point towards the pinky finger where I felt this. At times I felt kind of a strange hypersensitivity that would cause me to recoil my hand away from the stimulation of touch, kind of like when your hand or foot "falls asleep" and you experience that "pins and needles" phenomenon. Eventually I made a doctor appointment to have this checked out. Unfortunately, the sensation was not actively occurring when I went in for the visit, so I could only describe the problem and of course on examination they found nothing wrong. Ever had that situation where your car is acting up but on the day you take it to the mechanic its working fine?

Well, the sensations did keep coming and going and I began to lose the ability to discern what I was touching; for example, when I would reach my hand into my pocket to retrieve something I could not tell what I was grasping: whether it was keys, pocket lint, coins – they all felt the same. On better days where I did manage to tell if I had hold of a coin, I couldn't distinguish a dime from a nickel or a quarter from a penny. It was very frustrating! Symptoms never persisted on the days of a doctor appointment and they kept doing test after test. Then another strange sensation also began to happen; if I would bend my neck with my chin down towards my feet I would experience a tingling sensation that would originate from the back of my neck, down and out my arms and legs (kind of like a neurological electric shock sensation). They called this Lhermitte's Sign. They did an MRI brain scan and what was found was a small area on the surface of the left side of my brain that was absorbing an injected contrasting agent that is used to pinpoint possible areas of concern. The doctor said that it didn't have anything to do with my current symptoms because the sensations I would experience were in my left hand and this suspect spot was also on the left side of the brain. Let me explain: our brain halves deal with the opposite side of the body – the right side affects the left and vice versa. Anyway, the doctor wasn't overly concerned about this small spot just yet. He wanted it to be noted and to do another brain scan in a year to compare. Continued testing did indicate some abnormalities but revealed no clear answer for the occasional strange sensations in my left hand. Finally, the doctors gave up looking and said that this was probably something resulting from the extensive radiation I had received during treatment for my childhood leukemia. They said that I would just have to put up with this intermittent neurological "nuisance".

Well, at least I had the start of Bible school to look forward to...

Chapter 14

All in my Head

—◦◦◦—

As I prepared for Bible school I dedicated this upcoming time to God and expressed my desire to draw closer to Him, to seek His will for my life. I enrolled in the full-time course of study with a minor in youth ministry. I began to get very excited about the start of school; patience, Anthony, patience. I did not want to put those blinders back on. One thing I was learning was to keep focus on Him and He'd order my steps. Look at it like this: when a child is learning to walk they hold onto stationary things for security but when they venture out with first steps they can easily fall — every little thing can become a big distraction. However, when a parent is there to encourage them they'll stand a few steps away telling them to keep their eyes on them. When the focus is taken off the encourager they are easily overwhelmed and boom, down they go. The awesome thing is that all is not lost and soon comes, "Let's try again – keep looking at me". The steps are taken (with more falls, of course), then the race begins and the finish line is here before you know it.

On the first morning of classes we all gathered in the chapel for a meeting. This is how we would begin each day — together and praising God. Wow; very different from a secular college. I was going to like this. I surveyed the crowded room looking at the varied students mingling just before the service was scheduled to begin, and that's when I saw a certain girl. She was very cute, short like me and had a FULL head of thick, long, blonde hair; she intrigued me visually. Quickly I caught myself with a reminder of why I was there: to deepen my relationship with God and more clearly seek His direction for my life. I was there for God, not girls. Boy that was like a cold bucket of water over the head! The rest of the day progressed superbly — it was the start of something wonderful.

The year progressed...

I really enjoyed all of my classes and did very well academically and socially, I was making many good friends and memories. We often went out together to socialize in large groups. The blonde girl I mentioned from that first chapel service? Her name was Valerie, and she became one of my good friends too. As I got to know her more I fought with increasing feelings of fondness that were beginning to grow within me. I kept reminding myself of my primary objective for being at the Bible school, yet I didn't feel God cautioning me about feeling the way I was beginning to towards Valerie. Still, my painful shyness with girls kept me from revealing these feelings to anyone but my family and a close male friend at school. Valerie had no idea.

I guess my innocent revelation in casual conversation to my friend at school caused him to take a second look at Valerie because I watched as he seemed to hover around her more at school and during our group outings. I stewed in silence and paralysis, saying and doing nothing about it. Soon they were dating, and then one day in morning chapel, just after Christmas break, he announced that they were engaged to be married. I felt like I had been punched in the gut, hard. It was very difficult but I refocused on my studies and God. (Fortunately He was aware of my broken heart and the growing feelings of love I had held in silence.) Well, they ended up not marrying and she moved back home to San Jose before the school year ended. I thought I would never see her again. I gave my broken heart to God and trusted Him.

When I had gone home for the Christmas break, one afternoon the odd sensation in my left hand returned which had not occurred in quite awhile. When I called the doctor's office they said that I was due to have my follow-up MRI; a year had gone by. I had lost track of time; God hadn't. When this new scan was compared to the one from a year prior it showed that the spot on my brain had grown; it was a tumor. My concern about the weird numbness and tingling was put on the back burner as the focus was now on dealing with this meningioma tumor in the surface (dura) layer of my brain. The surgeon felt fairly certain that this tumor was not cancerous but that it would eventually cause problems because of its growth and the subsequent displacement of portions of grey matter. This would bring about a potential loss of normal functions. Brain surgery was scheduled to remove the tumor, and I was told I would face several weeks of recovery.

One thing I had finally learned was to place situations into God's hands, and I fully trusted Him for a positive outcome — this time it was not just lip-service. Brain surgery is a scary thing but I felt a peace that He was in control. Plus, because they'd be shaving my head for the surgery, I'd get to see how I'd look with a buzz-cut hairstyle once my hair started growing back. I had always wondered about this, it's all about perspective!

They performed a successful surgery and when I was coming out from the anesthesia, they told me that the sooner I felt up to standing the better it'd be for my recovery. They suggested that when the standing went well, maybe the next day I might try taking a few steps. Well, I felt good that afternoon and so I said I'd like to try standing, so I did. The hospital staff was very impressed with how stable I was. I was feeling ok with the standing so I said I'd like to try taking a few steps. They weren't planning on this for another day so they told me to lie back down if I began to feel uncomfortable.

Well, one step led to another and then to another. Everyone was amazed as I began to take a stroll up and down the hospital hallway. No one would have guessed that I had brain surgery earlier that morning! I felt good.

The next day I was approached by one of the doctors doing rounds with a group of medical residents. He asked if it would be ok for these doctors in training to interview me, an unusual patient. Pretty soon my hospital bed was surrounded by wide-eyed young doctors to be. They were all very impressed by my remarkable medical history and they wanted to know to what I credited survival and my exceptional ability to heal. Well they asked, and I was gonna tell.

I told them how I previously had plans to be a physician and that as a doctor you can bandage a wound but man doesn't cause the skin to heal; we do our part and God does His. I attributed my life to God; He was in control of my yielded life, not me. I encouraged them to not forget who brings about true healing. I had no answers for them other than that I trusted in God and believed in the plans He has for our lives, whatever the outcome.

My speedy recovery continued and in about a week I was sent home from the hospital to resume normal activities, including driving my car! As I continued to recover, I noticed that the numbness and tingling in my hand that was there prior to my surgery seemed to be gone. The doctor again reiterated that the tumor could not have played a part in those sensations (that whole left brain, left body thing —works conversely, remember?). Needless to say, I should be happy that they had stopped but that if any reoccurrences did happen they would probably be attributed again to my childhood radiation damage.

Still, despite this recent medical "setback" and scholastic absence, I returned to Bible school after a short absence and managed to finish that first year at the top of my class. This was another testament to God's hand working in my life. Remember my intellect was supposed to be hindered as a result of all that childhood radiation and the findings at the University in Davis where they said that I most likely had a learning disability?!

Well, first year graduation day came and as I walked toward the church for the soon to start ceremony, I was shocked to see Valerie driving through the parking lot. What a pleasant surprise.

After the ceremony she came down to speak with the first year graduates that she knew, and my heart leapt as she greeted me. I thanked her for coming back to the graduation and I totally misheard what she said next. She said she wouldn't have missed it, that she was proud of me. I *thought* I heard her say she wouldn't have missed it and that I was a part of her! This misunderstanding is what encouraged me to re-kindle our friendship and it's something we laugh about to this day. I guess I heard what God knew I needed to hear.

Valerie had previously moved back home to mend a broken heart after God told her to end her engagement. God was now encouraging her to move back to the Sacramento area that next year and to re-enroll back in the Bible school on a part-time basis. Our friendship started up again where it had been before it got side-tracked. She became one of my best friends and after several months I began to see her in the light of becoming a "girlfriend", but I still did nothing to encourage that because I knew she had been deeply hurt by her failed engagement and was still very scared of being hurt again. Add to that my painful shyness and our relationship flourished as nothing more than a deep, genuine friendship. Although I wanted it to be something more, I remained silent and patient. Funny thing is that close friends of Valerie could sense the growing bond between us, yet she remained steadfast in proclaiming to them that we were "just friends".

The turning point in our relationship came after a mentally ill man in Killeen, Texas drove his truck into a window of a popular, crowded Luby's Cafeteria in October, 1991 and proceeded to shoot customers before turning the gun on himself. He killed 24 people. At that time it was the worst criminal mass murder in U.S. history. I joined two other men from Capital Christian Center in Sacramento to help facilitate grief ministry to that devastated community. While I was there, Valerie found herself thinking of me often and genuinely missing my presence — she had grown accustomed to seeing me daily.

The day I returned from Texas I went to the church to surprise my friends at the Bible school and, of course, to see Val. She says that while I was gone she began to realize the strong feelings she was beginning to have for me. You know what they say; absence makes the heart grow fonder! She says that day when she saw me she was hit by a flood of happy emotions. I just kept trusting God to be in control of our situation and as that second school year progressed, we began to date. I'm not sure when things changed; it just seemed to transition naturally between us as time went on and on February 14th, 1992, I gave Valerie a promise ring. I promised that it would one day be replaced by an engagement ring. She was thrilled, and I was excited that she was ok with this. A few months later we went shopping for rings, and she picked one out that she really liked.

Towards the end of my second year at the Bible college, I was called in for a meeting with the school administrator (I hadn't done anything wrong, that I could remember, yet it still made me a little nervous like I was being sent to the Principal's office). I was told of a church that had let the college know they were looking for a youth pastor and the dean had thought of me as a possible candidate. What seemed odd was that this was an Assembly of God (AOG) school and the church that was looking was from a different denomination, not necessarily on the same page theologically with the AOG. The dean wasn't sure why this church had chosen to approach them for a candidate but that he knew I had come from a varied background and felt that I seemed to have a pretty grounded relationship with God; I focused on relationship, not religion or institutions. So, when he surveyed the student population he thought of me as a person who, with God's help, could handle this unique ministry opportunity. I was told to seriously pray about this and see what God would want from me regarding this. After I did, I felt led to make myself available to be considered for the position. The church voted for me 100% to come and be their youth pastor. You see, denominational labels mean nothing to me, what matters is your relationship with Christ (1 Corinthians 1:12, 3:4-9). I once had an awesome youth pastor who always said it doesn't matter what label you wear; it will either burn off on the way to Hell or blow off on the way to Heaven! Good words to live by.

I had decided I would propose to Valerie on her birthday in 1992. Two weeks prior to this date I told her that the ring she picked out had been sold, so we went ring shopping again. Before her birthday I wrote out a marriage proposal and found a Chinese Fortune Cookie company who made me a giant cookie and placed what I had written inside it. I then went to a local Chinese restaurant near where I was living and asked them to bring it out after her birthday dinner.

That evening they brought it out and she simply thought that a giant fortune cookie was just part of some Chinese birthday tradition. As she was excitedly trying to break apart the cookie, the paper with the fortune proposal began to stick out one side of it. My heart was nervously pounding inside my chest. I guess it was getting in her way because she pulled out the folded piece of paper and put it aside as she continued to try and get into the giant treat. I told her that you are supposed to read the fortune first before you eat the cookie, that this is the tradition and how it's supposed to be done. She looked a little disappointed as she put the cookie down and picked up the fortune. As she read it, her disappointed look was quickly replaced by a giant smile, just what I hoped. I presented her with the original ring she had picked out. Very surprised she said, "I thought you said the ring had been sold?!" My response, "It was... to ME!" Mission accomplished.

As we were planning for marriage I decided to get tested because I was not sure if my childhood leukemia had affected my ability to have children. Turned out that all the radiation I'd received had indeed sterilized me. I talked it over with Valerie to see how she felt about this and if she would still want to marry me. She said that if God wanted us to have children we would, it didn't matter what man said- and if not he'd give us peace. God has given me a very special gift in her! We were happily married on May 15, 1993 and remain so to this day!

Chapter 15

Living in my Calling

After graduation from Bible school and before my marriage to Valerie, I began my first "official" ministry position as the Youth Pastor at the community church I learned about at the Bible school. I was under the leadership of a wonderful man of God who affectionately referred to me as Anton (this was almost prophetic irony which you'll see later, keep it in mind). With God's guidance I was able to develop a thriving youth ministry in this church, and I felt like I was finally finding my "groove". I was also working part time as a receptionist at a professional building where I was living in Davis and I was managing a small apartment complex for my parents. One day an office building tenant asked me if I knew of any good automobile detailers in town. I told them I had not come across any but that sprucing up cars was sort of a love and hobby of mine. I offered that I could take care of whatever they needed on the weekend. When I brought the car back to them they were amazed. They said they'd had the car professionally detailed before but never had it looked as good as when I did it. I was encouraged to offer my services to others as a business of my own. This tenant was a graphic design and marketing firm and they went so far as to design a corporate identity for me. They created business cards and letterhead for me and even referred my first clients. Ah! Yet another hat for me to wear: Student, Apartment Manager, Receptionist, Youth Pastor, and now Automobile Detail business owner.

After close to one and a half years in ministry as a youth pastor at the little church in Sacramento, I began to feel an unrest within my heart. I began to feel that my time of ministry at this church was drawing to a close, which made NO sense to me. Things were going well — I had married Valerie, the young people were maturing, and our youth group was growing. I liked the people at church and they liked me. I ignored this feeling for a while, but I knew deep down that God was instructing me and I would find no rest until I obeyed.

I had to follow God's lead, and so I announced to the leadership and the church that I would be leaving. Of course the obvious question was asked, "Why?" I couldn't fully answer the question for myself other than I knew deep inside that this was God's leading and that I needed to choose to follow His prompting even without a complete understanding. It was a leap of faith. I knew that I had accomplished what God had called me there to do and I needed to listen to what was being put on my heart.

As I was going through this difficult time, I was reminded of what happened to me when I was a teenager in my own youth group. The youth pastor made the announcement that he would be leaving the position as our leader. It made no sense to me then, but now I understood with perfect clarity what he was going through. He spoke of how God had called him to lay a foundation for the group and now it was time for him to go and let the next person God had planned come to lead our group. God later gave me this practical example to see what was going on then.

We were close to moving into our first house and were blessed to see the stages of its construction. First the foundation was laid, upon which the whole integrity of the house would rest. The cement workers who built that foundation did an excellent job, but when they were done with their specific part it was time for the next crew to come who did the rough framing of the house. Next the roofers came to do their part and when they were done, the plumbing crew came to set the pipes.

Next to come were the electricians who did the wiring, then the drywallers, the carpenters, the painters, etc., etc., etc.; until finally the house was completed and we moved in.

Now what if we had become enthralled with the foundation guys and didn't want them to leave, I wanted them to construct the rest of the house, something for which they were not called and trained to do? Probably wouldn't have turned out to be as good of a house would it? Everybody has a specific role to play and a job to do (1 Corinthians 12). On the other hand, each craftsman could be wonderfully skilled but left alone to do whatever they pleased, whenever they wanted, that would be chaos — each person needs to be working off their specific set of plans in a certain timeframe. Fortunately, we have a Master Craftsman who is our General Contactor, and he has a brilliant schedule and set of blueprints for each and every one of us. We need to trust that He holds the Master plans. Again, I remind you of Jeremiah 29:11 (NIV), "For I know the plans I have for you," declares the LORD, "plans to prosper you and not to harm you, plans to give you hope and a future."

I was now excited for what was in store next for me and Valerie, and I excitedly looked for ministry opportunities in what would be our new hometown of Elk Grove, CA. I saw this as a new opportunity to minister within the religious denomination I was trained in. I contacted a small church in town, New Life Assembly, to inquire about a ministry opportunity. As it turned out, they were indeed in need of a youth pastor but for the time being it would be a non-paid position. No Problem, I had other sources of income and with God's blessing I felt I could make it until eventually this would become a paid position as the church grew. I was excited about the opportunity.

I figured I would do the same things I did at the church from which I was moving and that I would flourish and experience the same positive results; well it did not turn out exactly as I planned. I floundered for a year and a half at the church and found things to be about as productive as banging my head against a wall. My work with the youth there was not as it had been in my previous position. At the end of my time of futility I asked God why things were not working out, and this was the answer: He had placed me into my first ministry position, but I had placed myself into this second one. We won't experience fulfillment when we step outside of His will for us. At this point I felt led to resign from church ministry and focus my attention on the automobile detailing business that I had been blessed to start. It was going well.

I noticed something when I was a youth minister … people weren't always their true selves when in the presence of a "pastor". When visiting a youth group member's home I would always be introduced to their parents or other visiting adults as the young person's youth pastor, and immediately people would put on their best faces and watch their P's and Q's — I never got any real chance to touch their life and impact them on a real level, right where they were. Well, when I was in the business world, God allowed me to learn a valuable lesson: you see I thought that to be a "minister" you needed to have "Rev." in front of your name. Being a true follower of Jesus Christ has nothing to do with a title, a distinction, or what you say and everything to do with how you live your life. We are all called to be ministers of Christ's love to others. We are to preach the Gospel of Jesus always and if necessary to use words — I think it was St. Francis of Assisi who originally encouraged that. As an auto detailer there were no pre-conceived notions about who I was and people were themselves around me and I with them. After they got to know me I would find that some of my customers would just open up to me about different situations in their lives, sort of like a sounding board, not unlike bartenders (well sort of, minus the alcohol). I guess I was viewed as a neutral third party, just the "car guy" who wouldn't pass judgment and didn't run in their circles. I guess it was viewed that there was no need to put up a front with me. I hope God used me to sow some seeds of encouragement —- if not with words, with how I lived my life.

Chapter 16

A Progressive Illness Diagnosed

———

D o you remember the numbness and tingling sensations that I began experiencing prior to my brain tumor operation? It occasionally would come back into my left hand and then go away as mysteriously as it showed up; it was more of a nuisance than anything. In January 1996 I came down with the flu, and it hit me rather hard. I even ended up in the emergency room with difficulty breathing; seems I was so labored at times with my breathing that I would hyperventilate and my arms would gnarl in towards my torso as I experienced a lack of oxygen. This inadvertently triggered panic attacks that would then worsen my breathing which would then worsen the hyperventilating, a vicious circle that was broken only as I'd be encouraged to take slow deep breaths. However, one evening I started to worsen and developed a dangerously high fever of 105° which culminated in a late night ambulance ride to the emergency room. Seems my common flu was actually a serious case of influenza.

This too passed but I began to notice over time that I tired fairly easily and I seemed to be occasionally clumsy — tripping, falling down, and indiscriminately dropping things without warning. Over the next couple of years I adjusted to my new idiosyncrasies and tried to just get use to them. One day I began to feel coldness and numbness in the toes of my left foot. I kept seeing neurologists who would refer me from one to another trying to determine the cause.

Upon further exams they discovered that I had no pain sensation when my Achilles' tendon was pinched on the back of my foot above the heel. The neurologist that discovered this was with a medical resident who inquired as to why he found this unusual and he said, "If I pinched your tendon it would drop you to the ground, writhing in pain." There did not seem to be anything they could do for me; he said it was probably an inherited trait. I was given a diagnosis of having a neuropathy and it was suggested that I take a medication called amitriptyline to lessen the sensations. I was getting no real answers and was told to come back if my condition worsened. I was excited to at least have a diagnosis — I had a neuropathy. Then I learned that "neuropathy" is really only a generic term for an undiagnosed neurological phenomenon. The medication they wanted to prescribe does help with neuropathy, but I found it is a tricyclic antidepressant, something I did not want to take. I was not depressed and I felt I would just learn to get used to the cold toes and numbness. This condition with my left toes seemed to come and go like the sensations in my left hand. I did learn to deal with it; again, no real debilitation just a neurological nuisance.

As a result of my previous brain tumor it was recommended that I have regular, routine annual MRI brain scans to check for the appearance of any new tumors (a side-effect of all that childhood radiation). Well, I was diligent in doing this for many years, traveling back to the University of California San Francisco Medical Center (UCSF) for these scans (that's where my neurosurgeon was), but I eventually got side-tracked with other things in my life and missed a couple years of scans. I decided to get back on track and felt I could have a scan done in Sacramento with a local doctor. I kept trying to get my new local physician to refer this test but he didn't feel it was necessary as all my recent prior scans had come back clear. He felt that without any new symptoms it would seem medically unnecessary for my insurance to authorize further tests; he wouldn't even try. Well, I knew this was contrary to the wishes of my previous doctor, a neurosurgeon. I kept on requesting the scans and he kept refusing. I kept being persistent and he eventually ordered the tests. The resulting MRI brain scan seemed to concern him because it appeared to show multiple tumors. I was sent to discuss the scans with some local doctors. Finally, I decided to look up my original neurosurgeon from UCSF to discuss what these doctors were finding (the neuropathy and supposed multiple tumors). I was disheartened when they said he'd moved his office, but then I was thrilled when they said his practice moved to Sacramento (not far from where I was living at the time). I made an appointment for him to review the scans and he felt that what the others were seeing were not actually multiple tumors, most were old radiation scars. Most of what they noted had been there all along but were only now more clearly visible due to the enhanced resolution of newer MRI scanners. He did mention that there were two small suspect areas that were something he wanted to keep under watch. I mentioned to him the strange neurological sensations that were occurring and I questioned again if I might possibly have Multiple Sclerosis happening as well. Previous MRI scans suggested that I had some sort of demyelination phenomenon occurring; however when I brought this up he said he didn't suspect it was MS because there did not appear to be progression, and my

MRI scans never showed any new areas of activity. He said the scans showed the same things year to year aside from the new tumor occurrences and what he reiterated were most likely childhood radiation scars.

Here's the thing — if these symptoms were in fact due to a previously sustained radiation injury then it would stand to reason that they should not worsen past the nuisance sensations I'd experienced up to that point. Well, one evening the numbness and tingling sensations (known as paresthesias) returned to my left hand and since I'd gotten used to them and learned to deal with it, I proceeded to go to bed that night. A few hours into the night I awoke noticing that my left toes also felt numbness and the sensation seemed to progress up my left arm and leg as the night went on. Eventually I began to feel a tight banding sensation around my midsection; it kind of felt like a tire had been pushed down around my stomach. I woke up that morning and tried to stand up from bed to go into the bathroom but just fell to the floor because I had poor control of my left leg. I eventually made it to the bathroom and tried to brush my teeth and comb my hair but I had extreme difficulty when I tried to hold my toothbrush or comb in my left hand. My left hand and arm seemed to gnarl inward and as I looked into the mirror I thought I resembled a person suffering from Cerebral Palsy. I knew that whatever this was, it was not a static radiation injury but rather something active and progressing.

What is demyelination? The nerves in our brain and body are covered by a protein sheathing called myelin that acts to insulate our nerves and help facilitate nerve conduction. It's kind of like the insulation coating on an electrical cord that protects against short circuiting and helps the electricity get to where it needs to go. Myelin helps nerve conduction by keeping brain impulses flowing unimpeded along neural pathways to their final destination. Demyelination is degradation or damage to the myelin sheath. Something goes haywire in the immune system and it mistakenly thinks myelin is something foreign in the body that should not be there. With this attack, that is referred to as an exacerbation, comes inflammation that further adds to a slowdown of conduction (kind of like rubberneckers slowing to view a traffic accident). The attack can thin the myelin, leave holes in the insulative coating or, in extreme instances, sever the neuro pathway. The basic outcome is a "short-circuit" or misfire of the message from the brain to its destination and/or vice versa.

Well, now I was definitely experiencing worsened and new symptoms! I contacted one of my oncologists who treated my leukemia as a child. He knew of the previous radiologists' notations of a "demyelination phenomenon" but he also seemed to think that it was a result of radiation scarring. I told him of my new symptoms and my suspicions of MS, he suggested I could be seen at UCSF's Mount Zion Multiple Sclerosis center if I really wanted it looked into. I called them and had an appointment within two days.

Currently there is no single definitive test to diagnose Multiple Sclerosis. They base a diagnosis on the results of several different tests (sort of a process of elimination by determining what you DON'T have). They took an MRI scan while I was having these active symptoms; it showed areas of active lesions and damage. Their conclusion: I had an almost textbook case of Relapsing Remitting MS! This was March, 1999.

It seems that the smoking gun was the MRI scan done during an active attack because it showed new lesions. The follow up MRI looked like all the other previous annual scans. MRI scans always happened to be done previously when I was not experiencing any of my other "symptoms" which explained why no progression was ever seen. They started me on a course of intravenous steroids to help reduce the inflammation caused by the exacerbation. Over the next couple of weeks the control of my body improved and I pretty much returned to "normal". A follow up MRI showed no sign of MS activity (it looked like all my previous MRI's showing the unchanging radiation scars). The doctor who diagnosed my MS suggested I look into taking one of the FDA approved drugs shown to slow progression of the disease. I looked at two drug information pamphlets that were in the waiting area; both were interferon based medications that listed possible side effects like injection site reactions, liver damage, flu-like symptoms, and suicidal ideations among others. I knew my track record with treatments (seemed like all my medical problems stemmed from side effects) so because I seemed to have recovered for the most part I decided to not go on any drug regimen. At least now I knew what the underlying cause of my neurological "mystery symptoms" was. I could deal with this better now that I knew what was going on and my condition had a name.

After the steroid course to reduce inflammation from the MS attack, I seemed to almost fully recover and so I thought I would begin to function OK. I tried to resume life as usual and went back to my automobile detailing business. However, the first thing I noticed was that I did not have the stamina I had before. I previously had certain days where I could wash close to a dozen cars but now I felt the same level of exhaustion after only two cars. With the fatigue would come problems with physical motor control and I would begin to hunch forward as if someone were pushing on the back of my head (if I ignored this I'd eventually find myself on the ground unable to get up again until I rested for a solid 10-15 minutes). I knew that the future from this point on would be very uncertain, and I began to prepare my customers with the fact that the time may come when I would no longer be able to continue my business caring for their automobiles.

I faced a harsh reality one day as I was detailing a vehicle. I was polishing with a high speed rotary tool as I began to feel a loosening of my hold on the buffer. I consciously was telling myself to hold on tighter to this machine but it seemed the more resolve I had, the more the exact opposite began to happen. As my grip loosened, the polisher slid from my hands and bounced wildly down the hood while scratching the car's finish as it danced about. I knew that this was something unacceptable in this business and, so after repairing the damage, I decided this would need to be my last customer.

The $100,000 question: "What caused my M.S?"

Some researchers feel that a person can have a genetic susceptibility for developing MS and that the disease can be activated later in life by an environmental or possibly viral cause. Things like Mono, Varicella (Chicken Pox) and Flu strains are suspects. I have no knowledge of anybody in my family having Multiple Sclerosis so I theorize that it's possible that my susceptibility was artificially created by my exposure to radiation at an early age, during the formative stages of my immature immune system. Some medical researchers are suspecting a possible activating link between the Epstein Barr Virus and activation of MS susceptibility.

The Epstein Barr virus is more commonly known as Infectious Mononucleosis which I had a severe case of when I was 17. (Very close to when my first neurological symptoms began to evidence). I then had a severe case of chicken pox at age 18, then a serous bout of Influenza at age 27. That's my theory, anyway.

Chapter 17

Learning my Purpose

———

I made up my mind that I could no longer continue to be an automobile detailer because of my MS. Confused and disillusioned, I wondered what was I was going to do with myself now. For about a week I sat spinning my wheels while unsure of what would come next. Then I received a phone call from one of my commercial customers who owned an automobile collision repair center, he wanted me to work on a car in his shop that his employees had dirtied up. I told him that due to recent health issues I was no longer detailing. He asked if I would at least come down and advise his guys about what to do to remedy this particular issue. I reluctantly agreed.

While I was there, the owner began to quiz me on what was going on with me and so we spent some time talking. He asked me, "What now?" I told him that I did not know and that I was still deciphering what my remaining abilities were. He proceeded to tell me how he needed someone at his shop to manage parts for collision repair and that he'd love to let me try my hand at that. I told him that I had no experience with this and restated my uncertainty of my physical abilities. He said most of the work would be on the computer in an air conditioned office and that he knew I was intelligent enough to learn quickly. He was willing to give it a try, was I? Plus, he said he'd have other workers help me with the physical work like moving the parts around.

Well, that began my new stint as a body shop parts manager. My first day on the job I was unpacking a shipment of parts and was cutting the shipping straps with a brand new, very sharp knife. I nicked the first strap a couple of times to release it and then proceeded to cut the second strap with the same force, but I guess I must have hit it with a better angle because the blade sliced very easily through this second strap and into the thumb of my other hand while completely severing the tendon. I spent the next few weeks learning to do my new job with one hand. By the time my injured hand healed it was very easy to perform with two properly functioning hands. Also, as time went on, I was regaining some of the lost abilities suffered after the MS attack and so I didn't require as much help from other employees as I did at first (good thing because the shop was getting busier and it was getting harder to pull people away from their own responsibilities to help me). More than one vendor told me and my boss that I was one of the best parts persons the shop had ever had so far and that I easily was doing the workload of two to three people. I quickly realized a 50% increase to my hourly wage within months. I was happy and the owner was happy.

During this period of time my neurosurgeon was continuing to follow two new brain tumors that had been discovered. They had continued to grow and He said it was now time that they be dealt with. Due to the placement of these tumors he was not comfortable with doing traditional surgery on them like I'd had in the past because one was at the base of my skull near the spinal cord and the other was near an auditory nerve. One small slip and I could possibly end up quadriplegic and/or deaf. He suggested they be treated with a newer external beam radiation procedure known as Gamma Knife Radiosurgery. He just happened to head up a team that performed this new technique in Northern California! I had the one day outpatient procedure performed on March 9, 2000. The tumors' coordinates were mapped out using an MRI scan and then used to intersect over a hundred low dose pencil thin beams of radiation. By themselves these radiation beams are relatively harmless but at the point of intersection the radiation is very potent, enough to stop tumor growth and in a best case scenario even reduce size. A fixed titanium head frame is placed on the patient and secured to the skull by surgical screws. The radiation sources are embedded in a "helmet". The patient lays flat while coordinate adjustments are made to the frame. The table remotely slides until the frame locks into the helmet which is shielded from the medical staff behind what I believed was a lead door. It sort of reminded me of a large pizza oven.

My procedure went like this: doctors made adjustments to the head frame then left the room, the lead door opened and the table was remotely slid head first into the radioactive "pizza oven" where I baked for a few minutes. I was slid out, the door came down, the doctors came back in to make more frame adjustments, they left again, the oven door re-opened and this whole procedure repeated many times (I lost count). The whole procedure was relatively benign, and I was back to work after the weekend.

Things seemed to return to normal, but I began to notice that as time was progressing so were my responsibilities at work, along with my stress levels. I could sense that it was having a negative effect on my health, to what extent I did not know but I knew I needed to cut down my workload. I had previously talked with the owner about bringing another person on board for me to train to help with the parts, that the department was growing enough to warrant it. Unfortunately, this never seemed to get much priority.

I could feel internally that my health was starting to be like a ticking time bomb; I couldn't explain it but I could sense it. A couple of months went by and Valerie and I were preparing to go away for a weekend trip to celebrate our seventh wedding anniversary. By the end of that work week (a Friday) I decided I needed to make a decision regarding my work schedule so I met with my boss. I told him that beginning that following Monday I would be dropping down to a part-time schedule and if he would hire a candidate I'd begin to train them to replace me. I told him that this needed to be done as the stress of the job was beginning to have an effect on my health. He reluctantly agreed with me (of course, I didn't leave him with another option).

Excitedly, Valerie and I set out for our weekend excursion to visit a beautiful set of waterfalls in Redding, CA. We had reservations at a wonderful Bed & Breakfast Inn up there. We spent a glorious day enjoying the splendor of one of God's creations known as Burney Falls. As we were driving back to the Inn something very strange started to happen while I was driving. My vision suddenly became blurry and I began to see two of everything — double lane lines, double signs and double cars around us. Immediately I pulled over to have Valerie drive. I assumed this was maybe because I had over exerted myself during our trip to the falls; we did a LOT of walking on the trails.

Back at the room we took a little nap before going out to dinner. After a rest I seemed to be getting back to normal. The restaurant we went to that night was very dimly lit; I could barely see my dinner! I think it was steak, at least that's what I ordered and it tasted like beef. Nonetheless, it was good.

The next morning I opened my eyes again to double vision. When I sat up it seemed like the room began to spin violently and I felt nauseous — I barely made it to the bathroom before my previous night's dinner made a return visit. I wondered if I had gotten food poisoning, after all, I didn't really get a good look at what I'd eaten the night before! I laid myself back down but as soon as I sat up the room would again spin with a vengeance (kind of reminiscent of "Mr. Toad's Wild Ride" at Disneyland) and the nausea would return. We slowly went to the dining room for breakfast. Mine was a dish I had specifically asked for the day before but unfortunately I could hardly eat one bite. I felt so bad because the proprietor made it special for me, but I just couldn't do it.

The only way I experienced any relief from the nausea was if I laid flat curled up in a fetal position.

That is how I rode the entire long trip home in the back seat of the car while Valerie drove. Once home, I got out of the car and the spinning and nausea again quickly returned. My first emergency stop was the bathroom on the way to our bedroom!

The next morning Val made a rush appointment for me to see my doctor, which was a trip peppered with many nauseous pit stops. Eventually I found myself lying down, curled up on his exam room table. I was very confident in this doctor; he was the physician who uncovered my thyroid cancer over a decade before this. The doctor now gave me a brief exam and then proceeded to take my blood pressure as I was lying down, then sitting up, and finally as I stood (yes, you guessed it, I fought increasing nausea the entire time). He noted that my blood pressure decreased when I went from lying down, to sitting, and then even more when I stood up. He said this was the exact opposite of how it should be as blood pressure should increase when you change these positions in that order. Next he had me follow his finger with my eyes — this too was abnormal (something called nystagmus) as my pupils weren't tracking properly and they would bounce as I tried to focus on an object in my peripheral vision (to the extreme right or left, up or down). My pupils would do an involuntary, jittery movement. He told me that what-ever was going on, it was in my brain. He mentioned that I had been in his office about three months prior to get a general physical exam in preparation for a medical procedure; he asked what it was for. I told him that I had undergone Gamma Knife Radiosurgery to treat two brain tumors. He asked where they were and when I told him he immediately called my neurosurgeon to talk about what was going on with me. An MRI was ordered and it revealed something only millimeters from where the radiation treatment was done. He determined that the vertigo and nausea was most likely being caused by something called labyrinthitis, a condition probably related somehow to the Gamma Knife procedure I had undergone. I was prescribed an anti-nausea medication that didn't seem to help, and I actually would feel more nauseous shortly after taking a dose. The medication was subsequently changed with positive results (it seems that first anti-nausea medication was actually making me more nauseous! Go figure!!).

Well I had the vertigo and double vision for a long time. Needless to say I wasn't able to return to my job at the body shop. I remember that one day during the midst of all this, I was feeling a little depressed and decided to have a serious discussion with Valerie. I told her that I had assumed all my medical hurdles were behind me and that if I knew that there was still more to come I would not have done this to her by asking her to marry me. I knew that she didn't sign up for this and that if she wanted to end our marriage and go on with her life, I would understand; she was free to go. To my surprise and embarrassment she quickly put me in my place pointing to a large picture on the wall that we have that shows us standing on the church altar on our wedding day. She asked if I remembered standing there and making vows to each other to be together in sickness and in health. She told me that she meant what she said and that she wasn't going anywhere! She's told me that Multiple Sclerosis may change my physical body but it won't change who I am on the inside; THAT is who she fell in love with!

I spent a lot of time in bed for several weeks unable to walk without impaired balance. I couldn't read and trying to watch television was tiresome due to the double vision. Every morning I would awake, open my eyes and hope to see only the one ceiling fan above our bed. I was disappointed on so many days. A day finally came when I saw only one fan when I first opened my eyes but it quickly drifted into two images, gradually it stayed single for longer periods of time. Eventually I would enjoy single vision until I fatigued, then it would fade back out until I closed my eyes and rested. After a short recuperation my vision would improve but then worsen again accordingly as I tired. I was prone to getting dizzy and falling down and one of my doctors even described me as a being my own worst enemy and a danger to myself, it was suggested that I consider applying for disability benefits. I was very discouraged because my life was now drastically different — in my opinion it is probably psychologically easier to deal with a disability that you are born with as opposed to one you acquire later in life (you know you are different from the way you used to be and there is something tangible to miss).

With time my vision returned to normal while going double only when I was extremely fatigued and the vertigo subsided as well. I currently have problems with my walking; I have an abnormal gait and I experience problems with leg control. I also have difficulty with fine hand motor skills so typing this is very slow going, actually it's more of a hunt and peck style. My condition worsens with fatigue level and I tire *very* quickly. I now take medication to slow the progression of this disease. Who knows … had I started when it was originally suggested my second exacerbation might not have been so severe or left me with the neurological deficits and disability that I now experience.

One day in my past I was having a private time praying and talking to God. I started out by praying something I had often said, that I wanted God to reveal His will for my life and use me however He saw fit to use me and my abilities (although lately I wasn't feeling very able!). A thought flashed into my mind, "You are an excellent patient." This confused me at first and I wondered what this meant, but then I began to remember all the times God allowed me to exhibit His hand on my life in the medical arena; just the fact that I still endured in this life spoke of His existence.

My mind began to drift and I guess I was having a bit of a spiritual 'pity-party'. I began to mentally state my confusions, how I originally thought His will for me was to be a doctor but how that desire changed; then I thought His will was to be in youth ministry and then that changed; later it seemed He wanted me to be a businessman, well, that changed too; after that a Parts Manager in a body shop; now I found myself out of work and on disability! It seems everywhere you go people want to know what you do for a living – that's how the world wants to define you. I was now even more confused. God? How could I come so far from what I thought was my original intended purpose?!

"God I just want to know Your Will for my life!" I then heard God say to me (not audibly but as a clear thought in my heart), "You want to know My Will for you?"

"Oh yes, Lord, yes; that is what I desire!" was my internal response.

"My Will is that you know My Son, and that you make Him known."

It was so simple. I thought His will had to do more with a vocation — something dealing with a job or a calling since that seems to be how we are seen in this life; however, He showed me that our value comes from Him not what we do. I saw how we're the ones who over complicate things, not Him. He is our provider and our identity, not us.

A new statement surfaced as a question in my heart, "Why is it always about you?" "Sometimes I will use you to answer someone else's prayer and this in turn is answering your heart's prayer, which is, 'Lord, use me however You can'".

I realized He *was* using me, but when I didn't like where I ended up or if it didn't coincide with how I thought I should be used, I'd complain and 'shake a clay fist at the Potter' as the gifted musician Scott Abbott sings.

Like a slideshow in my mind, God began to show me how each season in my life had served His purposes. My leukemia led to my parents learning to trust in God (and how their sharing of that testimony has touched countless others). My desire to be a physician led me to Davis where I took the EMT course that led to my going to the doctor who was used to uncover my thyroid cancer which probably saved my life. This ended up with me fully surrendering my life to Jesus. A desire to be in ministry led me to Capital Bible Institute where I met Valerie; being a Youth Pastor gave me the chance to sow into young lives at a time possibly critical to their eternal future and for me to learn the lesson of not going ahead of God. Being in business taught me that every one of us is called to impact the lives of others around us, and that having REV. in front of your name does not make up the sole ministers of God's love in a dying world. How by being in that body shop, God allowed me to show the reality of a life truly changed by Christ to someone who had previously experienced hurt from those who professed Christ with their mouth but denied him by their style of life.

I saw it clearly; I had raised my sail and prayed for God to fill it; yet when He did I would find myself complaining about where the Wind of His Spirit had taken me.

God, forgive me.

Life at times is not easy, but the person that I am today is a result of the net effect of my life experiences so far. It keeps me in perspective, reinforcing the need for God in my life. I wouldn't change anything even if I could. I am grateful for everyday that God allows me to wake up and breathe the air of this life, I am truly blessed and you are too; don't ever forget that.

Here's a small additional side-note, another example of His undeserved mercy to me: One weekend I went with Valerie to visit some of her relatives in San Jose,

CA. As I was showering in the hotel bathtub I slipped, falling and forcefully striking my side on the edge of the tub as I fell (there was no bathmat or handrails). I ended up in the emergency room where they suspected I may have injured my spleen. After several hours and some tests, it was determined that I hadn't. The next day I had a horrible bruise and during the next few days a strange rash began to form on the injured area — I went to see a dermatologist and he said the trauma of the fall had caused me to develop shingles. He gave me a topical medicine to apply to the area; the rash began to respond to the medicine and eventually cleared up. The strange thing was that I had no pain other than the bruising from the fall. My understanding was that shingles is excruciatingly painful so I asked how this could be shingles when I had no pain. The doctor said that in a rare few cases of shingles there is no pain and so he guessed that I was one of the lucky few. I knew this wasn't luck ... this was a blessing!

Bible scriptures like this are a comfort to me when I feel discouraged; life is not automatically a bed of roses when you decide to trust in Him:

Romans 5:3-5 (NLT)
We can rejoice, too, when we run into problems and trials, for we know that they help us develop endurance.

And endurance develops strength of character, and character strengthens our confident hope of salvation. And this hope will not lead to disappointment. For we know how dearly God loves us, because he has given us the Holy Spirit to fill our hearts with His love.

James 1:2-4 (NLT)

Dear brothers and sisters, when troubles come your way, consider it an opportunity for great joy. For you know that when your faith is tested, your endurance has a chance to grow. So let it grow, for when your endurance is fully developed, you will be perfect and complete, needing nothing.

I now am learning to experience contentment wherever I end up in this life (at least sooner or later) — I have always and will always experience His hand on my life. I will fasten my seatbelt, keep my eyes on Him and enjoy the ride with the wonderful traveling companion He's given me in Valerie!

Chapter 18

Why?

———◦∞◦———

Icontinue to have daily struggles. I have good days and bad days living with Multiple Sclerosis but I try to look back only to see how far God has brought me. I know that each new day brings a new beginning so I look forward to and enjoy the good days while knowing and expecting the next when I have a rough one.

I'm thankful that I have had the experiences I've had as they have given me empathy for what others face. I've adopted the motto that if it doesn't kill me it will only serve to make me stronger. I joke with Valerie that the way things go in my life I should be able to give Arnold Schwarzenegger (when he was a body-builder) a run for his money by the time my earthly life nears its end.

I was officially told I have MS in March of 1999, but looking back I can see that the first undiagnosed symptoms started in 1989. I have experienced, first-hand, God's healing and I've learned that miracles can happen many ways; instantaneously, slowly over time, through natural means, and through medicine and the hands of doctors; these are all used of Him. I have at times had questions about why I still have to deal with this. I know MS is an easy obstacle for God to remove; so why hasn't He? I wish I knew the answer to that, but I've been given peace that He has been and will always remain in control of my life (that is if I allow Him to be, He is a Gentleman and never forces Himself on us). I have been told by several people that whether I realize it or not, people watch my life. This has made me think about the people who've told me that when they're having a tough time — they think about me and my struggles, how this gives them encouragement to persevere (funny, when I'm having a hard time I get my encouragement from thinking of others worse off than me who keep enduring).

This has also made me think of those who may look at my life with a critical eye and might say, "Sure, it's easy for *you* to have faith in God –- you've always received positive results when you or others have prayed for you!" I imagine that some others might look at this present hardship as my potential downfall. "This time

no answers are coming for the prayers, he's still sick —
watch, he'll grow discouraged and abandon his faith." I
think of how a person named Job in the Bible was told to
give up, to curse God and die! (Can you imagine? This
came from his wife!!) I will not give up! God has done so
much in my life and whether my healing comes during
this earthly life or when I get to the next in Heaven, I
have peace. My restoration will come either way, and if
this temporary suffering is now for the eternal benefit of
another then I count it a privilege!

Prior to my diagnosis of MS I was beginning to
make some overseas ministry trips where I had many
opportunities to share my testimony and what God had
done in my life. One place I really fell in love with was
Ukraine and its people. Remember earlier I mentioned
that I was a youth minister where the lead pastor called
me Anton? I later learned that this is a variation of my
name in Ukrainian! I really enjoyed these trips and could
see myself doing this more and more often, so you can
see how disillusioned I was when I became disabled.
This seemed to be yet another case of the devil trying
to discourage me and to pull the rug out from under
my feet. I am excited again because God has encouraged me that this book can go to more places than I
ever could on my own. This book will continue to share
about God and what He's done, long after I've taken my
last breath on this present earth. Future generations can

be encouraged and benefit from what He's has done in my life, even when it's over!

I learned somewhere that there comes a time when we all ask, "Why?" But even if we had all the answers, they still probably wouldn't satisfy our questions. We need to resolve to make a conscious decision that despite what ever comes our way, even when no suitable answers can be found… still we will trust in Him. God may not always prevent tragedies from occurring in our life, we need to accept that truth; but He can use them to deepen our compassion and ability to help others. We all will make it through this life to an eternity with Him if we yield to Him, but it is more fulfilling when we learn to stop and help others who have stumbled in the journey. This is not a race with a single winner; it is a marathon that we all must complete.

Sometimes when I look in the mirror I can't help but notice the physical scars from my medical past; Valerie calls them my 'battle scars'. What some might see as painful reminders, I've learned to see them as 'medals of valor' to be worn proudly; they remind me that I have an adversary who would like nothing more than to end my time on earth before more of God's glory is shown. We should remember the words in Ephesians 6:12.

These badges also serve as reminders of just how far God has brought me; Satan is a very real enemy, but I have learned that there truly is a God who loves me, and you, and the devil is no match. I feel a privilege that God's revenge on him is that I live. Strangely enough, one could almost respect Satan's traits of perseverance and tenacity; after all, without his efforts what would I write about? (Should I thank him? No, I don't think so.)

Chapter 19

Tomorrow? And I Thought I Was Done

—⟨∾∾∾⟩—

This book was heading for completion and almost ready for submission for printing when an unexpected medical hurdle arose this past year. I struggled with the question of whether this was to be an addition to this book or should be the seeds for a future writing. Well, I got my answer — I'll share a little of this most recent turn in my life's road with you now.

Well, so far I'd had three brain tumors treated previously when a fourth was discovered. This was just put under observation because it was slow growing and not causing any problems. In 2006 a fifth brain tumor was discovered and also put under observation. By the end of 2007 the latest tumor was determined to be growing significantly and would require treatment to stop it. In January of the next year I found myself at Stanford Medical Center to start an advanced treatment known by a rather ominous name — the "Cyber Knife". Actually, this is a procedure that involves no anesthesia, cutting, or sharp instruments of any kind. You lay on a table with your head immobilized with a custom fit mask made of a material that resembles the mesh stuff you put under a rug to keep it from sliding around. The mask is secured to a table while a pre-programmed robotic arm rotates around you, delivering short blasts of radiation at a predetermined target (in my case, meningioma tumors). Did you notice I used an "s" at the end when I wrote tumors? This is important to note, I'll explain...

The fourth tumor was just under observation because it had not grown much; however, one of the doctors involved decided it might potentially become a future problem so they would go ahead and treat it since they were already performing this procedure on me. I agreed with the reasoning. What I didn't think about was that they mentioned treating this tumor with a single, smaller radiation dose unlike the other tumor which was receiving its radiation dosage over three days. The reasoning for doing it in one day was for my "comfort" to lessen the amount of time I'd be lying on the procedure table. They said one day's treatment would suffice because it was a smaller tumor. I had chosen to do this CyberKnife procedure over GammaKnife, which I had done in the past, because it was going to be less invasive and done in smaller, multiple doses. I hoped this would reduce any shock to my immune system and lesson the odds of activating an MS episode. It didn't even occur to me that my oversight might be a risk.

It wasn't long after the procedure before I started having headaches, which I expected because the tumors swell slightly as they die before any shrinking in size. I experienced headaches after the GammaKnife, so I wasn't surprised when these began after this similar treatment. What I wasn't expecting, however, was the severity and frequency of the debilitating pain that emanated from the area of that single-dosed tumor. These pains were not helped by any of the remedies I'd used in the past and at times I sometimes felt like giving up and wishing I would die. I eventually ended up with pain management by several strong narcotic medicines. Unfortunately, I had to temporarily discontinue use of my regular Multiple Sclerosis medicine because of a counteractive effect with these opioid pain medications. I also took heavy and prolonged steroid treatment to try and reduce the swelling in my brain. The steroid caused me to retain fluid and I developed a very noticeable moon shaped face. I remembered having the "chubby-cheeks" as a five year old kid when I took steroids (prednisone) during my treatments for the childhood leukemia. The seven month combination of the steroid and the narcotic medications would cause my personality to take frequent and unusual turns for the worse that were totally out of character for me. The strange thing is that I'd have no remembrance when these episodes would happen. Valerie and my family exhibited the patience of saints during these times when I was "not myself"; their love for me is amazing. Amidst all this I experienced multiple infections while my health seemed to spiral out of control. I got a minor wound on my elbow which also infected and caused me to need surgery and subsequently a wound-vac before it healed up; the infection progressed and led to something called methicillin resistant Staph aureus, more commonly referred to as MRSA, which can potentially threaten your life. When you have MS, all these things happening was like poking a tiger with a stick, and I experienced what I dreaded from the beginning, a severe exacerbation. Something also happened with my bladder and I became incontinent. In a period of three months time from the onset of the headaches I became totally unable to walk. I required the assistance of others to do most everything as I could not support any weight on my legs or perform even basic tasks to care for myself. I had to be moved from one place to another such as a wheelchair to a bed, sofa, or into a vehicle and vice versa with the use of something called a slide/transfer board; I wondered if I would be facing life as a paraplegic. I longed for simple things that are often taken for granted like just going to the bathroom by myself. Valerie did her best in trying to take care of me at home but I was losing more and more of the ability to offer even minimal assistance with my transfers, bathing, toiletry, dressing and other daily activities. We came to the decision that I would require outside help beyond the scope of her, my family and friends. Six months after my treatment at Stanford I found myself in a care facility (where I quickly developed two bedsores and a change to a distended bladder that caused me to need a urinary catheter that they thought might need to be permanent. I eventually went to the hospital, an acute rehab program and finally wound up in a long term care center with skilled nursing and intense physical therapy. I can look back and see how in this whole journey each turn in the road was leading to a necessary destination. When I was at the first "care" facility I began to worsen in my condition rather than improve and when I needed to go for a medical appointment outside the facility I had a rapid onset of severe and sudden pain along with a severe bladder infection from the catheter — I begged the Dr. to put me in the hospital. After a quick trip to the ER I was quickly admitted to the hospital where they got me stabilized, placing my infections and wounds under proper treatment. By the evening of the third day

I was admitted into their acute rehab program. I began to make small but important gains with their therapy but I felt like I was only being prepared for living life in a wheelchair, as they were treating me like a spinal cord injury victim. In each facility I was in I had to be lifted from bed and transferred manually either by a couple of people or with a large powered lift which made me feel like an infant because it gave me the sensation of being in a large bassinette. Valerie even got training to operate one of these lifts because it was assumed that we would need one at home when the time came for me to be released (unfortunately this acute rehab was a short term program that would only last about two weeks). I did not feel ready to be going home so soon and Valerie felt the same way too. As I made new friends with patients at this facility I kept hearing a lot of them saying that they would be going to a longer term care and rehabilitation center nearby before they would be going home. We had not heard of this place so Valerie and I did some investigating to learn more about it and it sounded like exactly what I needed to give me more time for healing and gaining strength. We felt that this needed to be the next "pit-stop" on my road back home.

As it got closer to my discharge to the next facility, I began to want to sleep all the time and it felt like the advances in my condition were now retreating. I began to lose some of the abilities I had regained and it seemed like a reset button had been pushed and all my hard work in physical therapy was erasing. One day I felt a coldness that was chilling me to the bone, causing me to shake almost violently. A friend from the church we attended who happened to be a nurse at this medical facility was visiting that evening and noticed my symptoms seemed indicative of a low thyroid level (you see I need to take medicine to replace certain hormones since my cancerous thyroid gland was removed in the late 1980's). After a quick check she discovered I had not been getting this drug, an unknown oversight. I was about two weeks without this vital medication and as a result I had been experiencing the side effects of hypothyroidism. This explained my extreme fatigue, the decrease in functioning, and the intense feelings of being cold. I was placed back on my medication but unfortunately it would be weeks before I'd feel my thyroid levels normalizing.

I tried to prepare myself for what was to be the next part of my journey, to a place where I would actually spend over three months, initially lying helpless while flat on my back in a hospital bed. It seemed to me like my daily pills came by the handful. I even became, temporarily, an insulin dependant diabetic because of the steroid I had been on for so long. I was so heavily medicated with a regimen of drugs that I felt like I was the sole supporter of a small pharmacy somewhere. I spent countless hours staring at the ceiling while unable to move myself. Just sitting up seemed an impossible task. I depended on everyone else for everything; for some time I had reluctantly become adjusted to feeling like a rather large 39 year old giant infant. I had regressed to needing to wear protective briefs which are basically diapers and I couldn't clean, bathe, dress or feed myself. Every special person who cared for me during these very tough times was definitely an earth angel to me. I went nowhere unless someone took me there and I experienced severe crushing pains as the muscles in my legs were wasting away from atrophy because of a lack of use. I needed to be repositioned every two hours, including at night, because of the pain and my ulcerous but now healing bedsores. I spent what seemed like countless hours crying out to God, wondering what was happening to me and what I'd done wrong in my life to feel so forsaken. I prayed and wondered why God was silent, He isn't deaf or mute. I wrestled with desperation, depression, frustration, and at times confusing anger. I often would find myself in Valerie's arms just weeping. Pain was clouding my view of God. Still, I determined to keep trusting. Eventually, through it all, after A LOT of soul searching, I realized (and not for the first time in my life) that again there was no other choice than to release and abandon myself into His hands. His timing is not our timing, especially when He's raising us to a new level. I was learning a new lesson in perseverance, losing independence to better learn dependence on Him. Just before I left home and entered into "third party care" I had re-experienced a revelation of how intimately Jesus knows our pains because of *His* pain that was suffered for us. He was tortured and beaten beyond recognition; He was suspended by massive nails that were driven unmercifully through His hands and feet as He suffered a criminal's death on a cross even to the point of feeling separation from His Father God. Thankfully, He overcame. All this was suffered to ransom our captive hearts and provide a choice to live a life beyond this frustrating earthly existence, one where our veins course with a strange and poisonous mixture of Joy and Sorrow—Redemption and Sin. His blood was shed on our behalf to cleanse ours!

During time at the care center I eventually began to again feel a peace I can't explain (it's just experienced) and I re-realized God had never abandoned me, was always aware of me and that He is not the author of our hardships; He was there by my side even during times when I felt like He wasn't. With time I began to see answers to our prayers as I started to experience slow but steady improvements in my condition. With determination, I looked forward to each day as new progress happened. I was wheeled into that last facility and at the end I walked out their doors. I wasn't breaking any land speed records and it was with my forearm crutches, but I was vertical and under my own steam! I returned home on November 21, 2008 after a four month absence.

I am now able to care for myself in much of my daily functioning. I'm not back where I was before this last ordeal and life is slower, but God continues to sustain me; I wasn't killed and I'm stronger because of it (remember my adopted motto)! I look forward to what He will continue to do in and through my life.

So what's next? I honestly don't know, but I'm not worried about tomorrow because I know who holds my tomorrow, and with Him I can face whatever may come.

Do you know who holds your future? It's true peace.

Thank you for the honor and privilege of sharing a little of me with you!

After Thoughts:

My will vs. God's Will
A Lesson in Listening
By Valerie Rabak

—⟨⟨⟨⟨⟨⟩⟩⟩—

The Lord has taught me some invaluable lessons over the years, too. Here is where my story begins …

I moved from San Jose to Sacramento in 1990 to attend Capital Bible Institute (CBI). I didn't really have a ministry or career goal in mind. I did, however, have a heart for youth ministry as well as a desire for personal growth in my relationship with Christ. I had friends who had attended a year of study already, which is how I knew of this two year institute. I remember getting to know Anthony over the first few months; however, it was not "love at first sight" for me. In fact, I saw Anthony as the "class clown". He was fun, outgoing, entertaining … always quick in his responses to any situation with a humorous or, even sometimes, sarcastic remark. He was the fun-loving, best friend type. As he stated earlier, he never gave any indication to me that he had any interest in me other than that of a friend. Of course, I probably wouldn't have noticed anyway.

It wasn't long after classes began that I became side-tracked by the tall, cute, muscular guy in school. I was really taken by this particular individual and began to pray that if he was not "the one" that God would not allow anything to develop between us. I really did want the Lord's will in my life. However, I was young and had feelings for this person and rather than truly waiting on the Lord, we proceeded to date. Not only was he good looking, I just *knew* he was "the one" because of such obvious signs! Looking back, I roll my eyes at what those signs were: 1) He desired to be in youth ministry. I had always felt that one day I'd be a youth pastor's wife. 2) He drove a Honda Prelude! I had always wanted one of those!! Is this how God was providing me with a Prelude? 3) He had an older brother with Down syndrome. Being that I had grown up with family friends who had a daughter with Downs, I just *knew* this was another indication that God was directing this relationship. Girls, if your 'signs' are this super-ficial, they are not from God! In January 1991, after returning from Christmas break, our engagement was announced during chapel. It's important to note that one of the school rules was that students were not to date within the first year. This is not something that either of us even considered! Looking back, I can see what a red flag that should have been. I would highly caution anyone dating that if you are breaking rules to see each other, whether they be rules given by your parents or those within a school setting, you are **not** in God's will. He is the One who places people in authority over us; He is not going to direct you to then disobey them. If you can easily disobey your parents or those in authority, it can become easier to disobey Him! Proceeding while breaking rules makes for a very shaky foundation to build any relationship on.

Thankfully, the Lord snapped me to attention and in April I broke off the engagement. This was very difficult to do, as I stilled loved my fiancé, or so I thought! I did not want to break up and told God that if we were to end the relationship, my fiancé would have to do it. The instruction I received from the Lord was so definite that I knew if I didn't do it, I would be disobeying Him, which was not an option for me. I gave him the ring back and the next day, my hero, my daddy, rode into Sacramento on his "white steed" (his pick-up truck) and moved me back to San Jose where I could be with family and friends to mend a broken heart.

I remember being quite upset with God about my broken relationship but because I'd grown up in church, I figured it was terribly wrong to express those angry feelings. However, I finally one night cried out to God and expressed my anger. I was mad at God; why did He allow this to happen when I specifically prayed that He'd not let something progress if this guy wasn't "the one". I was a little startled to be corrected. God is a gentleman and won't force Himself on us, and He won't enforce His ways. I would've saved myself a lot of pain had I *listened* to the Lord rather than making it a one-way conversation! We can ask for the world, but if we don't wait for the answer, how is it fair to blame Him when things blow up in our face? He does have a way of getting our attention, but it's much less painful to give it rather than force Him to take action to snap us to attention. It was after this encounter with the Lord that true healing began to take place, and He was able to begin putting the pieces of my heart back together.

God's Will:

Returning Home

As the month of June approached, I knew that I wanted to drive up to Sacramento to witness friends graduate their first year, one of whom was Anthony.

One of my best friends and I took a weekend road-trip together and attended the graduation ceremony. As we were pulling into the parking lot, I spotted Anthony and another friend walking towards the church, and I honked excitedly so he'd know I was there.

The graduation ceremony took place as part of the evening service at Capital Christian Center. The honored guest speaker happened to be the pastor whose ministry I had had the privilege of growing up under at Bethel Church in San Jose. After so many years, I couldn't tell you now what he spoke about; however, his message spoke right to my heart that night and by the end of service, I knew that Sacramento was to be my home town!

My poor parents; God bless them! They had just moved me to Sacramento in September of 1990, back to San Jose in April 1991 and two months later, they were again moving me back to Sacramento. To top the move off, I had a waterbed at the time that my dear dad took down and set up each time! Thank the Lord for patient parents!

Just two weeks before breaking off my engagement, I had gone to work through a temp staffing agency at The Animal Protection Institute. In that short two week period, I had developed a friendship with my supervisor, June, and when I returned to Sacramento, she was willing to give me another chance; so, on July 1,

1991 I went back to work and remained there for five years! Oh how God provides! That friendship grew and remained strong for 16 years. We often commented that we might be sisters, and we were often asked if we were. As of this writing I have had to face the very unexpected death of June. At the tender age of 50, she had a massive heart attack and because of lack of oxygen to the brain, we lost her two weeks later. Anthony and I spent those two weeks by June's side, and her immediate family, praying, begging God not to let her die. I fully believed He could raise her up but for whatever reason, He chose to not heal her (in the way we would've liked). Life is anything but easy, and the difficulties we face can break us. This experience really shook me and my faith, and I struggled for many months with my "why" questions. I was even finally diagnosed with depression and anxiety after struggling for several weeks with ongoing heart palpitations. God is not surprised by our questions or anger; He just wants us to come to Him with it all. During this time I had to stand in who I knew God to be because I was not feeling his presence; to the contrary, I felt abandoned. But, I know God to be faithful, and his Word says that He will never leave or forsake us. He remains the rock we can stand on in difficult circumstances. Yes, we may have more questions than we have answers to but He is our only stability in an ever changing world, IF we allow Him to be.

Not only did I go back to my previous job, Anthony and I began spending more and more time together. Even though he had gone home for the summer months, he came up to Sacramento to see me on numerous occasions. In September, I enrolled back at CBI part-time and enjoyed having even more time with Anthony, who had quickly become my best friend. It wasn't until he left to minister in Killeen, Texas that I began to realize that I had developed feelings for him that were more than friendship alone.

He was gone for a week. I had grown very accustomed to seeing him or at least talking with him every day, so when he was gone I really missed him. I remember being at work one afternoon and getting a phone call from Texas. When I heard his voice, I was elated! It was after this conversation that I began to realize that maybe I was falling in love with this person but because I'd been so hurt previously, I was very cautious. After his return, we continued to spend a great deal of time together, but I would still report to friends and family that we were "just friends". In December, he invited me to join him to go visit his family; they were having a birthday party for his niece who was turning a year old. On our drive home, which was about an hour and a half ride, we were about 10 minutes from my home when he quietly asked me, "May I have the honor of holding your hand?" I was so surprised by this request that I said, "What?"

Thankfully, he did repeat his request, and I said, "Sure". So, for 10 of the 90 minutes, we held hands! It wasn't until years later that I admitted to him that I'd heard the question the first time but was so surprised that he'd asked. Poor guy had spent MILES working up the nerve to ask and then had to repeat it. Sorry, honey!

Things progressed in our relationship and as he shared previously, on Valentine's Day, 1992, he presented me with a promise ring and in September of 1992 he proposed. One of the great things that came as a result of my previous relationship and engagement was that when I fell in love with Anthony, I knew it was true love as what I had previously was infatuation at its best. I knew the love I had for Anthony was real, God-given and permanent. I remember while preparing for my previous wedding being told that "everyone has cold feet"; it's "totally natural". No; no it's not! When you are with the person you are meant to be with, according to God's plan, there is peace. That's not to say you won't encounter difficulty. The road from engagement to wedding was somewhat of a struggle with our families, but through it all we had peace that our union was meant to be, and we persevered. From engagement to the day of our wedding, never once did either of us question our decision or experience "cold feet". We feel and continue to be told that our marriage was "made in Heaven". If you are preparing to be married and have questions or doubts, please put on the brakes and don't proceed unless and until you have those issues resolved.

In Sickness & In Health

We were married in May of 1993 and in September, I was in need of a new car. After seven years wanting one, God gave me the desire of my heart as Anthony bought and brought home a 1990 Honda Prelude for me, a much better car than the previous Prelude I mentioned! I find this important to share for two reasons. First, as we walk in obedience to Him, He can give us gifts above and beyond what we ever even dreamed of! Secondly, although the type of car we drive is a rather insignificant detail, God does know the desires of our hearts, big and small, and if we seek Him first, He will give us those desires if they are in line with His perfect will for us.

Another desire I had all my life was to be a wife and mother. I wanted to have a child by the age of 30. When Anthony saw the doctor before we were married who told him he was infertile, I knew that if it was the Lord's will for us to have children, we would. Doctors are said to be "in practice", which some say means they are practicing medicine and do not know or have all the answers! God can and often does supersede what doctors say. This news was the first of many hurdles we'd have to face together.

In December of 1997, I went to work for *Christ for all Nations, the Ministry of Reinhard Bonnke (CfaN)* who is an evangelist to Africa. I am a firm believer that the Lord places us in certain circles for a season and for a specific reason. I absolutely loved my job and the people I worked with, but it turned out that I was not there for them; those people, who became my extended family, were there for me. It was while I worked at CfaN that our lives as we knew them began to change.

Anthony went for his usual MRI scan in 1998, and I hadn't given any consideration to the fact that something might show up as they were always negative. He had gone alone to the follow-up appointment when the scan was reviewed by his neurologist and after a couple hours, I began to grow anxious, so I called him. I asked him how it went, but he said, "I'll talk to you about it when you get home." Having to discuss something at home told me that something wasn't right, and it's not in my character to just accept that and finish my day. I asked him to please tell me what the doctor had said. As I sat alone in my cubicle, he proceeded to report that two tumors were found, one in the brain stem and the other in the left auditory canal. As this was told to me, I leaned over in my chair, resting my elbows on my knees as I cried. It was at this particular moment that my friend and co-worker passed by my cubicle and put her hand on my back and just started to pray.

When I hung up the phone, I told her what Anthony had said. She immediately gathered the entire staff into the conference room and because I couldn't speak, she told everyone about the report I'd just received. These precious people stopped everything they were doing and surrounded me as they began to lift Anthony and me to the Lord in prayer. How very sweet it is to know that we don't have to walk through valleys alone; God has placed special people in our lives to uphold us and help us on the journey.

As I drove home that night, I was really battling a feeling of being scared. My husband has brain tumors, one of which if not dealt with or handled properly could leave him paralyzed! I had the misconception that if I was scared, that meant that I didn't trust the Lord; however, I knew that I knew I trusted God to carry us through. So, how did being scared fit into the picture? I felt it was a lack of faith. I was listening to our local Christian radio station when a song came on that I hadn't heard in many years since hearing our church choir sing it in an Easter production. There's a line in the song referring to Jesus walking the path towards his crucifixion that says, "Then He walked through the gate, and then on up the hill…" At that very moment, the Lord spoke these words into my heart, "*I* was scared!" Boy did the flood of tears begin to flow! If Jesus, the Son of God, could be completely walking in the Father's will for His life and be scared, then how could we expect to do it any differently? Just like me, Jesus knew that He knew that God the Father would carry Him through; yet, He was scared having to walk the road He was on. That was such a blessing to me and allowed me the freedom to feel my human emotions while at the same time, trusting my heavenly Father to carry us through the valley. As I have recounted this memory over the years, I am not remiss in remembering that since that particular day, when I needed it most, I have not heard that song since! The Lord is so faithful to give us what we need right when we need it, if we allow Him to.

It was between 1998 and 2000 that Anthony also began to have symptoms that we would later come to realize as being associated with Multiple Sclerosis. As he shared, his doctors couldn't believe that on top of everything else, he could have MS; however, in doing his own research he found that to be the most likely cause of his difficulties. Okay; now he had two brain tumors that were being watched and a diagnosis of MS. I don't remember that either of us ever questioned God or got angry at Him. I do recall praying, "Lord, I know you can heal Anthony, but if you don't for whatever reason, please don't let his condition worsen." However, I have seen his symptoms progress and leave him with a level of disability that requires us to live in a way that others don't have to think about. When we go out, do we have his canes? Is his rollator (walker) or scooter in the car? Is the location where we are going handicap accessible? Is there a restroom nearby? Is the location air conditioned? One thing I miss the most about my marriage is being able to walk hand-in-hand with my husband, the man I love; my very best friend. He always has to either walk with arm canes or utilize his mobility scooter.

Yes, he has gotten worse over the years despite my prayers. Does this mean God has changed or doesn't care? Absolutely not. We are admonished in the Word of God, "And we know that God causes everything to work together for the good of those who love God and are called according to his purpose for them" (NLT). It doesn't say everything we face will be good; it says everything we face will work together for our good. Life isn't easy, but God never said it would be. We have learned to make adjustments in our lives and live with our limitations, and we continue to trust the Lord knowing that His love for us is GREAT.

Remember my desire to have children? That's one desire of mine that was not part of His plan for us. Age 30 came and went with no baby, and I had a time of grieving that loss in my life; not only for myself, but being an only child meant that I couldn't give my parents a grandchild. Turns out, in 2003 I was diagnosed with Stage III endometriosis and had to undergo a total hysterectomy. At the age of 33 I was thrown into surgical menopause and because of the endometriosis, I had to go three months without any hormone replacement therapy. I became best friends with my freezer as I'd stick my head in to cool off from the expected hot flashes, and those night sweats? Oh good grief! God knew that Anthony would have medical issues, and I would have physical issues limiting my energy. I struggle with migraine headaches, I've had an extensive history of kidney stones, and I have back problems. In God's gracious mercy, He knew that having to care for a child would make things so much more difficult. Although experiencing this loss of not being able to have children was painful, I can honestly look at our lives now and thank the Lord that we don't have children. I don't know how we'd do it. It's trying enough to take care of ourselves! Don't tell him I told you, but Anthony can be more than enough child for me at times!

Sometimes the desires of our hearts don't coincide with His plans for us, but His ways are so much better than ours. I'm so grateful He gave me the Prelude to enjoy and at the same time, I'm so grateful that He did not give us children. In retrospect, I am very grateful for the answer in both situations! He knows what's best, and He knows better than we do what we can and cannot handle. When we are in the midst of the storm, we can't see what He's doing or why He's doing it, but one day we can look back with 20/20 hindsight and be thankful for whatever the outcome.

I'm so grateful that the Lord does not give us a glimpse into our futures; oh the things we'd miss out on. Had He shown me that the man I married would become disabled after seven years of marriage, in my youth and immaturity, I don't know that I would've married Anthony; I can't say for sure. I loved him, but would I have "signed up" for life with limitations? I do know, however, that when I stood on the altar on May 15, 1993, I meant every word of my vows, including "in sickness and in health". The Anthony that I married is still the same caring, loving, funny, compassionate man of integrity that I promised to spend my life with. Yes he has physical limitations, but that hasn't changed who he is. If anything, it's made those qualities shine all the more.

My heart's desire now? I would love nothing more than to see Anthony healed. I desire to see him do all the activities he was able to do before his disability, and then some. If God should chose not to heal him, however, I know that I know there's a purpose in it, and He will carry us through just as He always has. I wouldn't trade these last 16 years for anything in the world. It is because of our trials that we have such a strong marriage, and our foundation in the Lord is so sturdy. We have learned so much about each other's character over the years, and we have learned even more valuable things about the character of our Lord that we might not have learned otherwise. His love is endless; His compassion never fails. Those are things that are of utmost importance. This life is painful, but in light of eternity, it's only a moment in time.

As Anthony shared, our 2008 was a very rough one and on top of having lost my friend, June, just the year prior I was more vulnerable than I may have been otherwise. What I found that I learned from June's passing is that my faith is very strong as far as believing that God can do above and beyond what we ask; however, there are times in which, for whatever reason, He chooses not do to things in the way we pray He will. This does not mean that we don't believe. I had someone who strongly stated that Anthony would be healed. When I questioned with a "what if God doesn't choose to heal him?" this person put a finger in my face and told me that if I didn't believe, then I had doubt. I felt like I'd been slapped in the face. If anyone believed that Anthony could be immediately healed and walk home, it was me; however, I also knew from recent experience that God does not always act the way we'd like Him to. He's not a genie in our bottle; He is God!

I have definitely had my weeping times with the Lord, yet I know that He hears my cry because after the mourning comes a joy that only He can give. He has given me peace that no matter what comes our way, I know that God will hold us close to His side and continue to be our constant gentle Shepherd. What our future holds, we don't know; but we know who holds us, and He'll never fail. For now, we buckle up and continue to ride this roller coaster we call life … together!

Here's to forever, my Angel! You will always be "the Wind beneath my Wings"!

Acknowledgements

I'd like to thank God, first and foremost, without whom none of this would be. Jesus, You're my Light. I'd like to sincerely thank all those who have encouraged me over the years to put God's workings in my life into print. Valerie, you are my best friend, true love, and partner in this life — thanks for being with me on this journey and for crossing my t's and dotting my i's. Next I want to mention my friends, Pastor David McFarland and Tom Pelster, who read and re-read the manuscript for this project — your thoughts and input are so appreciated. Pastor McFarland, thanks for being my teacher, counselor and one who performed the ceremony that married me to my best friend. Tom, thank you for shining the Light during a dark time in my life. To singer/songwriter, Scott Abbott, I appreciate you making me aware of my 'clay fists'; you are to be admired. I want to thank my family for the loving foundation you've laid for my life, for always being there for me to be strength in my weakness. I am fortunate. To my in-laws, thanks for raising such a beautiful woman to be an excellent part of God's plan for my life! Finally to you, the reader, thank you for taking the time.

To Contact The Author:

JustTellMeWhen@hotmail.com

If this book has positively impacted your life in some
way, please consider telling someone about it by
encouraging them to obtain a copy,
or give one as a gift.

CPSIA information can be obtained
at www.ICGtesting.com
Printed in the USA
FSOW01n0624220317
32175FS